WYCLIFFE AND MOVEMENTS FOR REFORM

AMS PRESS

NEW YORK

WYCLIFFE

AND

MOVEMENTS FOR REFORM

BY

REGINALD LANE POOLE, M.A.

DOCTOR OF PHILOSOPHY IN THE UNIVERSITY OF LEIPZIG.

NEW YORK

ANSON D. F. RANDOLPH & COMPANY

900 BROADWAY, Cor. 20th ST.

Library of Congress Cataloging in Publication Data

Poole, Reginald Lane, 1857-1939.
　　Wycliffe and movements for reform.

　　Reprint of the 1889 ed. published by A. D. F.
Randolph, New York, in series: Epochs of church
history.
　　Includes index.
　　1. Wycliffe, John, d. 1384. 2. Papacy—History.
3. Reformation—Early movements. I. Title.
II. Series: Epochs of church history.
BR295.P8　　1978　　　270'.5'0924 [B]　　　77-84729
ISBN 0-404-16129-4

Reprinted from the edition of 1889, New York
First AMS edition published in 1978

Manufactured in the United States of America

AMS PRESS, INC.
NEW YORK, N.Y.

PREFACE.

—+—

THE present work seeks to trace the history of the
different movements for reform in the system and in
the doctrine of the Catholic Church, which occupy a
prominent place in the interest and significance of the
fourteenth and fifteenth centuries. Except so far as it
deals with the life and writings of Wycliffe and with
the controversial literature of the age preceding his,
it makes no pretension to original treatment. In the
earlier chapters I have been permitted to embody the
substance of several passages in my *Illustrations of the
History of Medieval Thought* published in 1884 by
the liberality of the Hibbert Trustees; and in the
latter part of the book I am under large obligations
to the works of Professors Creighton, Loserth, and
Maurenbrecher. I regret that I have been prevented

57953

by illness from giving to the final revision of the book that amount of care which is due both to the importance of the subject and to the kind consideration of the Editor of the series; but I trust that the oversights due to this cause will not be found to be numerous.

REGINALD L. POOLE.

JESUS COLLEGE, OXFORD,
Christmas 1888.

CONTENTS.

—⧫—

CHAPTER III.

The Popes at Avignon—The Papacy and England.

CHAPTER IV.

The Early Life of John Wycliffe.

CHAPTER V.

Wycliffe and English Politics.

CHAPTER VI.

Wycliffe's Earlier Doctrine.

CHAPTER VII.

WYCLIFFE AND THE GREAT SCHISM.

CHAPTER VIII.

LOLLARDY IN ENGLAND AND BOHEMIA.

CHAPTER IX.

THE DIVIDED PAPACY.

CHAPTER X.

THE COUNCILS OF PISA AND CONSTANCE.

CHAPTER XI.

JOHN HUS.

CHAPTER XII.

THE END OF THE FIRST REFORM MOVEMENT.

CHAPTER XIII.

RELIGIOUS REVIVAL IN SPAIN AND ITALY.

CHAPTER XIV.

Reform in Germany : The Lateran Council.

MOVEMENTS FOR REFORM

In the Fourteenth and Fifteenth Centuries.

———+———

CHAPTER I.

BONIFACE THE EIGHTH—THE PAPAL POSITION.

THE Reformation of the sixteenth century was partly a religious, partly a political movement. On the one hand it was a revolt against the supremacy of the Pope of Rome; on the other, it was a restoration of what were believed to be the doctrines and practices of primitive Christianity, as distinguished from those which had grown up in the Latin Church since the time when it had begun to have a separate existence from the Churches of the East. Of the two motives for reform, the former was at the beginning most commonly the prevailing one; but in a short time they became indissolubly united, and it became as impossible to conceive of a Church departing from the Roman obedience without modifying its doctrinal system, as of a Church which should admit these doctrinal changes and yet remain faithful to Rome. This was because the Reformation was soon seen to imply not merely the acceptance of this or that political or theological doctrine,

Political elements in the Reformation.

but a revolution of a more vital and penetrating kind. It meant in fact the destruction of traditional 'authority,' as authority, saving only that of the Bible; it asserted the dignity of the individual man, not solely as a member of an ecclesiastical system, but as an independent being with his own religious concerns to look after: briefly, it substituted the modern for the mediæval conception of man and of society.

How far or how logically these two principles of the right of private judgement and of individual respon-

Traceable in earlier times. sibility were carried into effect by the protestant reformers, it does not fall within the plan of the present work to inquire. All we have to do is to search through the weary centuries that witnessed the decay and collapse of the mediæval order of things, for vestiges of a striving towards something more vigorous; and we shall not find mere vestiges, mere presentiments, of the new spirit. No great movement ever takes the world quite by surprise; if a revolution is only a *coup de main* its success is sure to be transient. Neither the opposition to 'authority,' nor even its application to Christian doctrine, was by any means the discovery of the Reformers of the sixteenth century. The general principle had been firmly thought out more than two hundred years earlier—to go no further back,—and from that date there was an unbroken succession of writers in its defence. Their aim was indeed almost entirely directed against the Papal power; for them, authority was, as it were, embodied in the Papacy. But before the end of the fourteenth century Wycliffe had extended his line of attack to some of the special doctrines of

Western theology; and the movement which he began, though its effects were evanescent in his own country, became in the hands of more stimulating advocates a genuine national force in Bohemia. Still, the slightness of the hold which Wycliffe's doctrinal innovations, as distinguished from his ecclesiastical protestantism took upon men's minds, is significant of the fact that in this respect he did not represent any very widely spread feeling of discontent. It was not as yet the accredited doctrines of the Church, but the abuses in its external system, that aroused antagonism. Wycliffe's popularity was won, and his influence was maintained, by virtue of his assault upon the Papal power; and it is to such opposition as his,—essentially a political opposition, involving the familiar antithesis of Church and State,—that the beginnings of the Reformation are to be traced.

We have by implication dated our starting-point about the time of Boniface the Eighth, an epoch which is rightly accepted as marking the crisis when the ascendency of the Papal power was checked and when its decline began. Since the fall of the house of Hohenstaufen, which rapidly succeeded the death of Frederick the Second in 1250, the Empire had been left without an occupant. After a long interregnum and a disputed election, the German crown was possessed by a succession of rulers who did not aspire to be more than kings of Germany. The tradition of universal sway which had animated their predecessors had for the moment passed out of mind. There was a danger that it might be revived in the hands of the Pope, whose admitted universality

Epoch of Boniface VIII. (1294–1304).

of spiritual power was apt to be interpreted by himself as implying a divine right over temporal rulers; and no time could be more favourable for carrying this claim into effect than that in which the great rival of the Papacy seemed to be once for all extinguished. Such a result was hindered by the rise of new political forces of which it had not previously been thought

National opposition to his policy, necessary to take account. The opposition between the Church and the Empire was in truth changing into a general opposition between the Papacy and the civil governments of the different kingdoms. France and England were growing fast in solidity and national feeling; and under Philip the Fair and Edward the First they were strong enough to make a stand against what they deemed the encroachments of Pope Boniface. England no doubt was placed in an unfortunate position

in England, for such a purpose, in consequence of the tribute which still remained as a token of her subjection to the Roman See; but when Boniface attempted to interfere in Edward's dealings with Scotland, the Parliament of Lincoln met him by a peremptory assertion of the king's absolute independence in

1301. all temporal concerns: 'The kings of England neither have been wont to answer nor ought to answer, touching their rights in the said kingdom, or any other temporal rights, before any judge ecclesiastical or secular, by the free preëminence of the state of their royal dignity and of custom irrefragably observed at all times.'[1] The vigorous action too which Edward had taken in regard to the clergy,

[1] Walter of Hemingburgh, Chron. 2. 212.

when Boniface by his famous bull, *Clericis laicos*, prohibited the exaction from the clergy of any taxes or subsidies from the revenues of the Churches, may serve as evidence that John's surrender to Rome was not held to involve anything beyond a monetary obligation upon his successors. The very tribute was generally in arrear, and at length in the time of Edward the Third and under the advice of Wycliffe, who wrote a state-paper on the subject, it was expressly repudiated by Parliament and never paid again.

1296.

But it was with France that the decisive struggle took place. In that country the clergy had previously enjoyed immunity from taxation, so that when Philip the Fair called upon them to bear like burthens with the rest of the inhabitants, it was natural that the Pope should intervene in their behalf. Whether or not directly provoked by Philip's exactions, the bull *Clericis laicos* certainly followed promptly upon them, and was met by open defiance on the part of France. The details of the contest do not concern us here; but it is important to notice how the King's imperious will enforced itself upon the whole French people and made the struggle a national one. To understand the way in which this came about we have to bear in mind the process of consolidation which had been going on in the French monarchy and administration through the thirteenth century. A leading characteristic of the age is the legal spirit which prevailed not in France only but throughout the west of Europe. In the earlier years of the century the Emperor Frederick

and France.

1296.

the Second had been legislating for Sicily; at the
end of it another Frederick had carried on the same
Growth of the work in that island.   The laws of Alfonso
legal spirit,   the Tenth of Castile, of Lewis the Ninth of
France, and of Edward the First of England, are all
symptoms of the general tendency towards systema-
tising and codifying law.   In France this tendency
had been accompanied more than elsewhere by the
especially in   rise of a distinct and powerful class of
France.   lawyers.   Philip the Fair raised them at
once into a position of new importance when he expelled the clergy from all part in the administration of
the law and made the civilists supreme in the courts.
In the lawyers Philip found his stoutest and ablest
supporters, and it was thanks to them that he succeeded in carrying with him the general. approval of
the nation.   For the lawyers were not a mere faculty
at Paris; their profession dispersed them over, and
established them in, all parts of the realm.   They not
only filled many of the municipal posts, not only did
they hold civil jurisdiction everywhere, but they had
even appropriated part of the legal business and jurisdiction of the churchmen.   Through their instrumentality then the whole of France was made cognisant
of one side of the case in dispute between Philip
and Boniface; to support that side became a point
of patriotism.   The clergy, whose interests had been
injuriously affected by the rise of the lawyers, might
have been disposed to advocate the opposite party.
But this does not appear to have been actually the
case.   The Gallican clergy had always prided themselves on their national privileges.   They were by an

old tradition less closely dependent upon the Roman
See than the clergy of other countries; and we do not
find that as a body they resisted the policy
of Philip the Fair. Some did, no doubt;
others were frightened into a passive
acceptance of established facts: but a great number
shared actively in the national zeal which was aroused
by, and which steadily supported, Philip's defiance of
the Pope.

National character of the support given to Philip the Fair.

It is this national character which gives the French
conflict with Boniface the Eighth its historical importance. When, in 1301, the Pope declared
that Philip held his realm of him, and
cited the king to appear before a council
to be convened at Rome, the bull was publicly burnt
at Paris. Philip then summoned the Estates-General
of France for the first time in its history to express
the national agreement; just as Edward the First
had summoned the first regular and representative
Parliament seven years before, in order to prepare
against a pressing national danger. The Estates-
General met in April, 1302, and drew up their remon-
strance, each order separately,—the nobles, the clergy,
and the commons,—in the form of letters to the cardinals and to the Pope. Boniface took their letters
into consideration in a consistory which he held at
Rome in June. The result of these deliberations was
the issue towards the end of the year of the bull
Unam sanctam, a bull which takes its place beside
the bull *Venerabilem* of Innocent the Third, and the
Clericis laicos of Boniface himself, among the decisive
acts of the Roman Pontificate. The bull *Clericis*

Outline of his contest with Boniface.

laicos merely defined the claims of the Church with respect to immunity from secular taxation ; the bull *Unam sanctam* asserted uncompromisingly the supremacy of the spiritual over the temporal power in all relations : ' We declare, assert, decide, and pronounce, that it is necessary to salvation that every human creature be subject to the Roman Pontiff.' Negotiations between Rome and Paris were attempted, but with no success. Philip was excommunicated, and in reply

June, 1303. solemnly arraigned the Pope before his Parliament. He caused an appeal to be read before it, in which he promised his efforts to have a general council summoned in order to carry into effect the deposition of Boniface. The assent of the Estates having been given, the appeal was confirmed by no less than seven hundred acts of adhesion from bishops, chapters, monasteries, the several orders of friars, and the University of Paris.

Emissaries of the French King were meanwhile in Italy. They professed to be working purely for the pacification of France and the Papacy ; but their real

September 7. object became evident enough when they appeared at Anagni, where Boniface was residing, attended by a body of armed men, hired chiefly from the neighbouring and rival city of Ferentino. An attack was made upon the palaces of the Pope and of the cardinals. They fled and hid themselves ; only the Pope remained dauntless. His life was spared, but he was subjected to an ignominious imprisonment for some days. At last he was rescued by the people of Rome ; but the outrage he had suffered was too much for a man of eighty-six years to

endure. He died in a month, of a fever, or, as some
say, madness. The catastrophe which befel him, absolutely without precedent in the history of
October 11. the Popes for centuries past, led directly to
the humiliation of the Papacy under the shadow of
France. After a short interval,—the uneventful pon-
The Popes in tificate of Benedict the Eleventh,—a Pope
exile. was elected through French influence, the
first of the line of French Popes. Clement the Fifth
fixed his seat in France, and then just across
1305. the border at Avignon, where it remained
until 1376. The return of the Papacy to Rome
was quickly followed by the Great Schism
1378. which was not finally healed until more than
half-a-century after.

The Babylonian Captivity,—as the Papal sojourn at
Avignon is called,—and the Great Schism, each in its
own way, produced a current of feeling in Western
Christendom which threatened to be fatal to the old
theory of the universal supremacy of the Pope. At
Avignon he sank into the position of a mere French
ally, and was in consequence exposed to the same
sentiments of national hostility which the action of
France aroused in other countries, such as Germany
or England, towards herself. After the schism, when
there were two or, it might be, even three Popes, the real
position of each was separated by a still greater distance from that which he claimed to hold. And when
at last union was restored to the Papacy, the process
of disintegration in the allegiance, of weakening in
the affections, of Western Christendom had gone too
far to be arrested. The head of the Church by this

time had given up reform as hopeless; it was enough
if he could maintain the state of things as it was:
and so little vigour was left in the system that when
the Protestant revolt was raised, it seemed for a while
as though the entire ancient order was doomed. That
the Catholic Church after all survived, and, what is
more, that it recovered its vitality and won back
much that it had lost, was due to the fact that it at
last itself set to work in earnest to reform its internal organisation. Had it done so a century or
two earlier there might have been nothing lost to
need winning back.

The opponents and the advocates of the Papal prerogative in the fourteenth century adopted a different
mode of warfare from that which was cus-
tomary in earlier times. Controversial
pamphlets and letters had always been
written on either side; but now a controversial literature comes into existence which bases itself less upon
the occasional questions of the moment and more upon
general principles. It takes a broader view of the
nature of the State and of the relations of the temporal
and spiritual; in a word it seeks to lay the foundations of a political philosophy. It is this literature
which gives a special interest to the ecclesiastical
disputes of the period; but in order to understand its bearing we must first glance at the position held by the Papacy, as it was and as it claimed
to be.

First, as the head of the Church, or, as he had
now come to call himself, the *Vicar of Christ*, the Pope

*Changed char-
acter of Church
controversy.*

assumed the right of summoning general (that is, ecumenical) councils and of confirming their acts. Papal claims. The council advised, but he claimed not General only to originate its decrees but to give councils. them a ratification without which they were invalid. It must not be forgotten that formerly the power to summon such councils had been held to be a part of the imperial prerogative, or at least a right to be exercised by the Emperor and Pope conjointly.

Secondly, the Pope had extended his direct control over the Italian and then over all metropolitans, and Ecclesiastical finally over all bishops ; since upon the for- preferments. mer he conferred the *pallium,* the symbolic token of their office, and the election of the latter was apt to be insecure without his confirmation, though this was not legally necessary. If the Pope made no positive assertion of a right to dictate the election of a particular person to a bishoprick, his request, or, as it was now termed, his *mandate,* amounted in some countries to a compulsory nomination. Besides this, he exercised the power of deposing bishops and of translating them from one see to another. The *annates,* or fees payable to the Roman court on collation to a bishoprick or abbacy, which it was afterwards attempted to extend to the case of every sort of benefice, formed an important part of the Papal revenue ; and the practice of repeatedly translating prelates, so as to multiply the occasions for such payments, became a favourite device with financially-minded pontiffs like John the Twenty-second. The freedom of election asserted for the English and other Churches thus came to have little meaning.

In the third place, appeals to the Pope were encou-

raged in causes of the most various kinds and from a
constantly increasing sphere of jurisdiction.   It would
be unjust to deny the abstract nobility of a

Appeals.

conception which sought to erect a supreme
court of appeal high above all earthly considerations.
But the Papal Curia, with whatever justice, was generally suspected of partiality, corruption, even direct
venality; and the evils with which these appeals were
attended,—the tediousness of the procedure and the
frequency with which appeal followed appeal, while
parties were restrained from action until the last appeal
was decided—had long been a standing source of com-
plaint with the more conscientious clergy.

Fourthly, the Pope claimed a universal power of
absolution and dispensation.   This is implied in the
famous phrase of his *plenitudo potestatis.*

The *plenitudo potestatis.*

In the words of one of the greatest and
most thoughtful supporters of the hierarchical theory,
Saint Thomas Aquinas, ' the Pope hath the fulness
of power in the Church, in such wise that whatsoever
be enacted by the Church or by the prelates of the
Church is subject to dispensation by him.'   This definition covers all matters of human or positive law,
and only excludes matters belonging to the ' law of
nature ' and articles of faith.[1]   But according to other
authorities, and possibly, in one place elsewhere,[2] to
Saint Thomas himself, not even articles of faith were
exempted from the Pope's power of alteration, though
not of dispensation.

Fifthly, the Pope claimed the right of exacting taxa-

---

[1] Thom. Aquin., *Quæstiones quodlibetales,* vi. 13.

[2] *Secunda Secundæ,* i. 10.

tion from the Churches of Christendom.   How far this
claim was actually enforced varied, of course, with the
circumstances of the different countries.

Taxation.

In France, for instance, even though the
Pragmatic Sanction of 1269 be now rejected as a
forgery, it was frequently denied ; in Castile, on the
other hand, by the enactment of Alfonso the Tenth,
soon to receive the sanction of law, it was expressly
conceded.   In England, which ranked theoretically as a
fief of the Holy See, the right was incessantly and
oppressively exercised.

Sixthly, for the past two centuries and more, the
custom had been growing up of sending legates from
the Pope to enforce both his fiscal and his

Legations.

judicial claims over the different countries.
The legate superseded the authority of the national
clergy and held provincial councils as the Pope's
representative.   Even in England, where the Archbishops of Canterbury from the time of Stephen
Langton were regularly appointed legates, the mission
of a special legate (*a latere,* as it was termed) was held
to override the prerogative of the permanent officer.

Seventhly, the Papal power had received an enormous extension from the codification of the Canon
Law.   This body of prescriptions is of a

The Canon
Law.

very composite origin.   The so-called Isi-
dorian Decretals, a great part of which was forged in
the ninth century, though professing to be a genuine
collection made by Isidore of Seville at the beginning
of the seventh, had rapidly won general acceptance ; but
various interpretations of them had come into existence
among the lawyers, and it became desirable for a text-

book to be arranged which should compare and reconcile these discordant glosses. This text-book was the
work of a Benedictine monk, Gratian, in the middle
of the twelfth century ; and the *Decretum Gratiani*,
in three books, forms the *first part*, the basis, of
the authorised *Corpus Iuris Canonici*. But opportunity was soon found for further explanations and
distinctions, the most important of which were consciously directed towards the enforcement of a higher
doctrine of the Papal prerogative. In the earlier
decretals there was a good deal that, instead of supporting, stood in actual contradiction to the theory of
the Papal power as it became gradually developed ;
and accordingly the later portions of the *Corpus Iuris
Canonici* were written not merely as a commentary
upon, and a supplement to, the *Decretum Gratiani*, but
also to no small extent as a corrective to the imperfect
doctrine therein contained of the rights of the Papacy,
—a doctrine by no means satisfactory to canonists of
the type of Gregory the Ninth. It is to this Pontiff
that we owe the *second part* of the canon law-book,
or, more accurately, the first five books of it. The
work was done at the Pope's command by a Dominican friar, Raymond of Pennaforte, in 1234. A sixth
book was subsequently added by Boniface the Eighth
in 1298 ; and, to conclude the series, as the traditions
and usages of the spiritual courts grew in bulk with
the growth of the Papal assumptions, new supplements
were authorised by Clement the Fifth in 1308, and
by John the Twenty=second in 1317. These two
supplements are known as the *Clementines* and the
Extravagantes. The *Extravagantes* (divided into two

books) were thus named because they were intended to meet difficulties and obscurities 'running outside,' that is to say, not resolved by, the previous collections.

By these stages grew up a body of laws, and as a natural result a body of lawyers, expressly devoted to the maintenance, the consolidation, and the enlargement of the powers and privileges of the Church as against all temporal authority, and of the Roman See as against all authority temporal or spiritual whatever. The autocracy of the world, the *plenitudo potestatis,* is now centralised in a single power and in one person ; that is to say, by its own theory, expressed in its own law-book. The acceptance which it met with, so far as it touched temporal interests, was by no means so unequivocal or so universal ; and the history of the two centuries following Boniface the Eighth is the history of how this hierarchical theory broke down in practice.

Before this time the Papacy had received an immense accession of strength by the foundation of the mendicant orders, the Friars Preachers and Friars

The friars.   Minor,—black friars [1] and grey friars,— better known by the names which have been given them in modern times from their founders, the Spaniard Saint Dominic and the Italian Saint Francis of Assisi. In earlier centuries the monastic system had once and again been reformed and vitalised by the creation of new orders, or by the establishment of houses affiliated to the older houses and distinguished only by the greater purity and greater strictness of their discipline. Such had been the Cistercians and the Bernardines,

---

[1] By mediæval writers the Dominicans were often called Jacobites, from the dedication of their great church at Paris.

offshoots of the Benedictines; and the new orders of
the Carthusians, and the Carmelites: all of which
originated between the last twenty years of the eleventh
century and the middle of the twelfth. Their increase
was checked by the action of Innocent the Third, who
in the Lateran Council of 1215 expressly forbade the
establishment of any new monastic order, 'lest too
great diversity of practice should bring serious confusion into the Church of God.' Of quite a different
character were the two orders of mendicant friars
which arose almost simultaneously in the first quarter
of the thirteenth century. They were unlike any order
before them; they were unlike any sect. Both setting
forth with a missionary purpose, the band of Preachers
organised by Saint Dominic devoted themselves to the
work of counteracting heresy and error, and of drawing
over the heathen to the Christian faith; the Friars Minor,
led by Saint Francis, sought more directly to revive the
life of Christ and his apostles, and to bring the civilis-
ing influences of Christianity to bear upon the neglected
populations of the towns, the rapid growth of which
had left large regions destitute of spiritual oversight.
Soon these orders were joined by the Carmelites, who
adopted the Franciscan rule in 1245, and by the
Augustinian hermits, whose order was founded in
1256.[1] While the monks practised their discipline
with a view to their own personal advancement in
the religious life, the friars bound themselves to, and
trained themselves by, an even stricter rule, with the

[1] It is hardly necessary to warn the reader against confounding these
Austin friars with the Augustinian canons, whose rule was established in the eleventh century.

single object of devoting the virtues thus acquired to the good of others. They dwelt not apart from the world, but in its midst; for many years, in conformity with the founders' injunction, they had no house of their own. They lived on alms, and took no thought for the morrow. The sole aim of their work was to root out error and to plant the truth.

This is no place to describe the extraordinary beginnings and progress of their enthusiastic career. For the present purpose it is only necessary to observe that the unmeasured popularity won by the friars was directly serviceable to the Papal policy. By the privileges conferred on them by the Popes they were made absolutely independent of the bishop and clergy of the diocese in which they might choose to settle themselves, and subject alone to the See of Rome. The mendicant orders thus formed, as it were, the Pope's standing army, free from all control of the local spiritual authority. Diffusing themselves everywhere, they extended with their influence the high doctrine of Papal autocracy. The favour with which they were received gave them the last thing contemplated by Dominic or Francis, wealth; and enabled them to depart completely from the original conception of their order by providing themselves with splendid houses and establishments. The Franciscans, too, and after their example the other orders, had auxiliary branches of unattached members, called Tertiaries, who observed the general principles of the rule in a sort of lay-capacity, and were equally pledged to the furtherance of the main objects of the society.

At the same time it is needless to say that these

Their relations to the ecclesiastical system.

powerful organisations were not so favourably received
by the local clergy whose domain they invaded. Between the friars on the one side, and the secular clergy
and the monks on the other, hostility was almost inevitable; and as the mendicant orders declined from their
original nobility of aim and practice, it followed naturally that the opposition directed against them should
recoil upon their Papal patrons. Their demoralisation
furnished a motive to some of the earliest and most
bitter attacks of this kind, which were carried on in
an uninterrupted course through Wycliffe down to the
time of Luther. Nor was it only classes external to
the orders which undermined their position. Among
the Franciscans there early arose a party holding more
closely to the pattern of their founder than the mass of
the order was inclined to do; and between these and
their fellows an implacable strife was waged. It is
in fact this quarrel concerning the obligation of observ-
ing 'evangelical poverty,'—or the absolute rejection
of temporal property according to the practice, it was
deemed, of the Founder of Christianity and his apostles,
—that originated the first controversies in the Middle
Ages of what may be termed a conventional Protestant
character. To these we shall come in their proper
place. It is here only important to note that while
the rise of mendicancy was a mainstay of the Papal
power, its decline was closely connected with exaspera-
tion against that power. The date at which this
decline is first clearly manifested, the date at which
the first serious convulsion within the Franciscan body
took place, corresponds with the pontificate of Boniface
the Eighth and the 'spiritual' propaganda of Peter

Johannis Olivi. Still the 'spiritual' party among the Franciscans was never, except for a short time during the pontificate of John the Twenty-second, more than a minority; the great mass of the order, as of the other orders, continued to be the devoted allies of the Papacy.

In these various ways the Roman See maintained and augmented its ascendency, commanding, or at least claiming to command, all the kingdoms of the earth; it had come to interfere even in the internal affairs of the different states. Its spiritual position needed however to be confirmed by temporal sovereignty as well. For the greater its exaltation, the more striking was the contrast between the proud attitude of the Papacy towards foreign nations, and its personal insecurity or even helplessness in Rome itself. The mightiest of the Popes might be driven from his seat and die, as Gregory the Seventh died, in exile. It was thus inevitable that the Papacy should seek to establish itself in security by the acquisition of a territorial domain. Its spiritual arms might be potent enough to overpower resistance abroad; at home the Pope must perforce be also a temporal prince. By the time of Boniface the Eighth the Papal dominion extended all along the western half of Middle Italy, from Tuscany to the borders of the Neapolitan kingdom, besides detached possessions in other parts of the peninsula.

Temporal sovereignty of the Pope.

The necessity of such a temporal domain at once reveals the point of weakness in the mediæval theory of the Papal autocracy. When the Church in the eleventh century undertook the task of reforming itself in order that it might reform the outside world, it went upon the principle that, the sharper the distinction, the separation, between clergy and laity, the more readily could the former be brought to bear, as an external and consolidated force, upon the disorders of the civil society. If the Church was to exercise its due sway over the consciences of men, it was felt that it must be as free as possible from the ties which bound it to the secular State. If, for instance, the Churchman had to look to his king alone for preferment, he was not likely to be as vigilant or as courageous in the carrying out of his duty as if he depended solely upon his spiritual chief. The independence of the clergy being thus postulated, it was but a step further to assert their superiority, their right of controlling the State. Gregory the Seventh professed to have discovered evidence in the Papal archives which satisfied him of the direct feudal dependence of the different kingdoms on the Roman See.[1] He founded his supremacy on a plain principle, namely, that all earthly power was the invention of worldly men, ignorant of God and prompted by the devil : it needed not only the assistance but the authorisation of the Church.[2]

A political view like this evidently made demands on the clergy which could hardly be satisfied in a much more advanced stage of civilisation. It is needless to dispute whether it was right or wrong ; it is quite enough that it was too ideal and visionary. As soon as it was brought into the sphere of practice,— so soon as the Church entered into conflict with the

---

[1] Epist. vi. 23 in Jaffé's *Monumenta Gregoriana*, pp. 46S f.

[2] Epist. viii. 21, *l. c.*, p. 457.

State,—it became clear that the unworldliness assumed in the Church only existed in so far that it had no material forces to rely upon ; although the weapon of excommunication which it wielded was in fact by far more formidable than any forces that the secular State possessed. If the clergy were free from civil control, society on the other hand had scant protection against their license. To make the high ecclesiastical officers proudly independent of the sovereign, was to introduce the influence of the Roman See into every court, and to put canonical obedience in danger of becoming a matter of common politics. If ecclesiastical property was released from civil obligation, the Church was as much as before subject to the cares and the temptations of wealth. The spiritual basis of the hierarchical pretensions in fact speedily broke down on trial. The Pope in aspiring to universal dominion fell to the position of a sovereign among sovereigns ; he busied himself in the acquisition of large territorial possessions: he became a disturbing influence in the political system of Europe, and the most devout of Churchmen were constantly troubled to reconcile their duty towards their country with what they believed to be their duty towards God. The direction therefore in which the Church had been tending for more than two centuries involved elements of danger not only to society but to the Church itself; and it becomes a matter of peculiar interest to examine the modes of argument by which it was attempted, in the interest of the Church, to draw it back to a purely spiritual position.

CHAPTER II.

THE FRANCISCAN CONTROVERSY—MARSIGLIO OF PADUA AND WILLIAM OF OCKHAM.

WHILE the contest of Pope Boniface the Eighth with Philip of France opened the political struggle which undermined the ascendency of the Papacy, the contemporaneous internal dispute among the Franciscans marks the date at which churchmen began to realise the injury which Christendom was suffering from what they deemed the mistaken policy of the Popes. Each of these controversies has a literature of its own, a literature in which there are many signs of a wider interest than the mere technical, often trivial, points actually in dispute. But we must here confine ourselves to the Franciscan controversy; for it was this which contained the seeds, and more than the seeds, of the debate as to the nature and functions of the Church, which gave substance to future movements in favour of reform.

We have already noticed that within not many years of the foundation of the order, and in direct violation of its principle, the Franciscans had allowed themselves to receive endowments of enormous extent; they had their convents and their estates, and seemed to be turning into something not unlike a new order of monks, while completely surpassing them in

Divisions among the Franciscans.

popularity. The question then arose, on what tenure they could hold this property without contravening the terms of their profession. Urban the Fourth solved the difficulty by the ingenious explanation that the friars could only enjoy the usufruct of their possessions; the actual proprietorship of them belonged to the Pope. Nicolas the Third, however, in 1279, in the bull *Exiit qui seminat,* expressly enforced the doctrine of absolute poverty as an essential element in the Franciscan rule. This bull was inserted by Boniface the Eighth in the Sixth Book of the Decretals, and thus became the established law of the Church. But the bull lent itself to various interpretations, since it allowed the friars the ' moderate use ' of earthly possessions; and it was this question of interpretation that threatened a disruption in the order.

The stricter school was represented by Peter Johannis Olivi, who died in 1298. His followers were consider-

The extreme party.

able in number. Many of them adopted the rule of the hermits founded by Pope Celestine the Fifth, giving up the Franciscan discipline as too free for their ascetic needs. The Celestinians were severely treated by Pope Boniface and the order was suppressed; but the spirit infused into its members remained powerful and extended itself among the regular members of the Franciscan order. Clement the Fifth tried to heal the breach by an authoritative declaration of what the Franciscan rule meant; but his bull *Exivi* did nothing more than repeat what

Nicolas the Third had laid down about the distinction between property and use. The Spirituals under Ubertino da Casale were bidden under pain of excommunication to return to the obedience of the order.

The reason why the Popes took such severe action against them has been found in the fact that their Repressed by the Popes. assertion of the duty of poverty implied a censure upon the licentious and prodigal life of the Papal court; but in truth their doctrines were connected with various theological tenets which were directed against the very existence of the hierarchy, tenets which foretold the downfall of the existing system and the substitution of a purer and more spiritual order of things. Visionaries these men doubtless were; but they lived in an age which was only too ready to carry theories into practice, and in practice their spiritualism proved the vigorous ally of Ghibellinism. Some of the opinions of Olivi were condemned by the Council of Vienne in 1311; the sanction of Christendom was given to the policy of Pope Clement. Nor did John the Twenty-second fall short of the rigour of his predecessor in his treatment of such dangerous sectaries. He found the Dominicans willing enough to help him, and their special engine, the Inquisition, was set to work in several parts of France. For a time the Pope was assisted also by many of the regular Franciscans and by their general himself, Michael of Cesena. The points which were condemned in the bull *Gloriosam ecclesiam* of January the 23rd, 1316, centred in the assertion of the Spirituals that there were two Churches, —the carnal one, rich and profligate, which was

governed by the Roman Pontiff and his court, and the
spiritual Church, whose 'kingdom is not of this
world,' represented by the friars of the extreme
section. The two parties within the order lived on
until in the latter half of the fourteenth century the
reformers acquired a recognised position under the
name of Observants, as distinguished from the Con-
ventuals, who were freer in their interpretation of
the founder's rule.

In the meantime, in 1321, a new period in the
history of the controversy began; and a new party-
division came into being which must be
Question of
'evangelical
poverty.' carefully kept apart from the movement
led by the Spirituals, although both ran on
parallel lines and both were at one in their antagonism
to John the Twenty-second. This new schism originated in a specific point of dogma. The question now
was, not whether the Friars Minor were bound to observe their vow of poverty, but whether Christ and
his apostles ever themselves held any property. A section of the Franciscans maintained the negative; and
if Christ and his apostles never possessed anything
whether privately or in common, the inference was
irresistible that neither could his successors, the whole
body of churchmen, hold any possessions : ' evangelical
poverty,' in the technical phrase of the controversy,
must be the law of the Church. In 1322 a chapter
of the entire order was assembled at Perugia, and the
doctrine of evangelical poverty was formally accepted.
Michael of Cesena now stood by them, as did also the
representatives of the order in other countries, including
France and England. Pope John replied by accusing

the Franciscans of heresy; the Dominicans and the University of Paris added their voice to the Papal condemnation. The Franciscans, however, held their ground;—they were now reinforced by the powerful advocacy of the great English schoolman William of Ockham:—but the Pope would not flinch from the necessary conclusion of his acts. He annulled the bull of Nicolas the Third and asserted that 'use' was inseparable from 'proprietorship.' The Franciscans in their turn accused the Pope of heresy; but repeated threats soon reduced the main body of the order to obedience. Still an influential minority, commonly but loosely known as the Fraticelli, continued firm. It was at this juncture, when the Franciscans, the old allies, the very mainstay, of the Papacy, were at open variance with Pope John, that a number of them resolved to throw in their lot with the German king, Lewis of Bavaria, and to seek by his instrumentality to carry into effect what they believed would prove the means of the regeneration of the world.

The momentary results of this singular combination of forces can here be only glanced at in a few words.

The Friars and Lewis the Bavarian. In 1324 Lewis had been excommunicated by the Pope; but the German people held loyally to their King, and he resolved to make good his title by a coronation at Rome which should make him no longer a mere German sovereign but the successor—if only in theory, still the legitimate successor—to the universal Empire of the Romans. Lewis's Italian expedition was really organised and controlled by his Franciscan allies, though the greatest champion of their views was, it happened, a secular clergyman, Marsiglio dei Raimondini, lately a respected teacher in the University of Paris. To Marsiglio and to his Franciscan fellow-workers is due whatever of principle and of permanent historical significance belongs to Lewis's scheme to rescue the Empire from the unendurable pretensions of John the Twenty-second, and to reassert for it a power and dignity such as even in the strongest days of the Franconian or Swabian emperors had been proved totally incapable of lasting vindication. Lewis's career in Italy was short and inglorious. He became for a moment master of Rome, was crowned by two excommunicated bishops; an Antipope, Friar Peter of Corvara, was chosen, and Marsiglio was named Papal Vicar in the city. But Lewis, like most emperors, found himself quite unable to maintain himself long at Rome. He retired to Pisa, and here was joined by Ockham. Michael of Cesena was also in his train. We need not linger over the inevitable collapse of the whole undertaking. The Antipope made his submission at Avignon in 1330 ; the spring of the same year found Lewis again in Bavaria, his hopes in Italy not only unrealised but destroyed.

January 1328.

Still for some years he kept up a vigorous paper-war with the Pope. The scholars and theologians on whom he had rested remained true to him. ' A strange international colony,' as it has been well described,[1] now established itself at Munich. ' Parisian professors, and Italian, English, and German friars constituted, with a few native statesmen and ecclesiastics, the political

[1] Riezler, *Die literarischen Widersacher der Päpste zur Zeit Ludwig des Baiers*, p. 76 (Leipzig, 1874).

and theological council of the Emperor.' Within not
many years the majority of them were frightened back
into the Papal obedience.   Lewis himself long sought
a reconciliation; but often as he made offers of subjection, and though at one time in 1343–4 he nearly
succeeded by humiliating sacrifices in obtaining what
he desired from the Pope, now Clement the Sixth, he
continued under excommunication until his death in
1347.   Of those who as long as they lived worked and
strove for him the most memorable names are those of
the two Parisian masters, Marsiglio of Padua and William Ockham; and it is their writings which show us
the new turn which political and theological opinion
was taking, the new ideas of Church and State which
were silently making themselves felt.

Marsiglio's chief work, the *Defensor Pacis*, was written
in 1324 while he was still at the University of Paris,
though he must then have already meditated a union
with the German King.   Professedly a treatise written
with a view to the establishment of a firm peace between the spiritual and civil powers, it is in fact a
sustained argument for the supremacy of the latter
within its own sphere : and it is much more than this ;
it announces a clear constitutional system such as in
the present day either exists not at all or exists only
in name in the greater part of Europe.   Its author
was one of those rare philosophers to whom fortune
gave, as we have seen, the opportunity of carrying
their conceptions into practice; who discovered also
that, however capable of constructing from the foundation, they were powerless to reconstruct in face of the

old-established and irreconcilable facts of society with which they had to deal. That Marsiglio's active work was a failure lay in the nature of things : his real importance is to be found less in the events in which he was of necessity precluded from exercising paramount control, even had he been able to exercise it with the desired success, than in the book of which those events were so impotent illustrations.

To secure peace, this is the motto of the political treatises of Marsiglio's day. A French lawyer in the year 1300 was sanguine enough to expect that this end might be attained by the submission of the world to French rule ; for, he says, ' it is a peculiar merit of the French to have a surer judgement than other nations, not to act without consideration, nor to set themselves in opposition to right reason.' [1] A few years later Dante, in his treatise *De Monarchia*, had sought to establish universal peace by the restoration of one universal State under one supreme ruler. Less ambitious, though for his age not less unpractical, Marsiglio discovered the remedy in a definition of the province of the temporal and of the spiritual estate, and in a limitation of the latter to strictly spiritual matters. The boldness of such a statement will not be directly apparent to those who are unfamiliar with the immense extension which had been given to the word ' spiritual ' by the usage of the Middle Ages. But the originality of Marsiglio's general view of the

The *Defensor Pacis*.

[1] See the excerpts from the *Summaria brevis . . . felicis expeditionis et abbreviationis guerrarum regni Francorum,* no doubt the work of Pierre du Bois, given by Natalis de Wailly in the *Notices et extraits des manuscrits,* 18 (2) 435-494 (1849).

nature and functions of government will become clear
at once from a short sketch of his leading propositions.
He does not rank with ordinary imperialistic partisans;
still less are his principles at one with those which
prevailed among civil lawyers. That which he insists
upon as the very basis of the social organism is a
maxim which they were inclined altogether to ignore.
The sovereignty of the State, he maintained, rested
with the people; by it properly are the laws made,
and to it they owe their validity. If the making of
laws were entrusted to a few, we should not be secure
against error or self-seeking : only the whole people
can know what it needs and can give effect to it.
'The community therefore of all the citizens or their
majority,' expressing its will either by elected representatives or in their assembled mass, is the supreme
power in the State.

But it must have an officer to execute its behests,
and for this purpose the people must choose itself
a ruler. In Marsiglio's view election is the only
satisfactory means; to the hereditary principle he
will make no concession whatever. There must be,
he says, a unity in the government; but a unity
of office, not necessarily of number : so that the
executive functions may be as effectively exercised
through a committee as by a single prince; only no
member of such a committee must venture to act by
himself separately, its policy must be directed by the
vote, or by a majority, of the entire body. If however,
as is usually the wiser course, a king be chosen, he must
be supported by an armed force, large enough, according to the rule of Aristotle, to overpower the few

but not large enough to overpower the mass of the nation. But this force is not to be entrusted to him until after his election, for a man must not secure the royal dignity by means of external resources, but by virtue of his own personal qualities.

The desirability of a universal monarchy Marsiglio leaves altogether an open question. He is as little disposed to magnify the pretensions of the German King to whom he dedicated his work, as he is to admit any theory of the indefeasible prerogative of kingship as such; prerogative indeed, strictly speaking, the king has none, for the authority which he receives by the act of election is purely official; the 'fountain of justice' remains with the 'lawgiver,' the people, whose instrument he is and to whom he is responsible. He has to interpret the law, not to make it. So too the officers of the State derive their commission from the people, albeit the king, in conformity with law, decides the detail of their appointment, together with the other necessary arrangements of the executive government. Once establish the principle, and the conclusions are easy to draw. The king's power is limited in every possible direction. He has the eye of the people or of its representatives on all his actions. He may be restrained or even deposed if he overpass his prescribed bounds; and even though his conduct be not amenable to the letter of the law, he is still subject to the final judgement of the national will. On no side is there any room for despotism; in no point is he absolute.

In treating of the different orders of society, Marsiglio finds that one,—that of the priesthood,—presents special difficulties. For whereas the peculiar province of the clergy is to instruct the people according to the teaching of the Gospel with a view to their eternal welfare, they have so far abandoned this exclusively spiritual office as to usurp all manner of temporal claims over temporal as well as spiritual persons, and in particular over the Roman Emperor: and these pretensions of the Papacy are the chief causes of discord in the world. Marsiglio therefore proceeds to examine the real nature of the spiritual office, and of its relation to the civil State. The name *Church* he would recall to its first and apostolical, its ' truest and most proper,' signification, as comprehending the entire body of Christian men : all, he says, are alike churchmen, *viri ecclesiastici*, be they laymen or clerks. It is intolerable that its prerogatives should be usurped by the sacerdotal order. Excommunication, for instance, cannot rightly be decreed by any priest or any council of priests : they should doubtless be consulted with reference to the charges alleged, and it is for the priest to declare the sentence ; but the verdict belongs to the ' community of the faithful.'

Marsiglio's idea of the Church.

While moreover the clergy have no right to engross the name of churchman, they have also no right to apply the word *spiritual* to all they do, as when they use it to protect their property and incomes from legal burthens or conditions. The clergy have indeed a spiritual office in the Church, but their general dealings, their tenure of land, their financial and other temporal engagements, are just as much worldly as are those of their lay brethren, and just as much subject to the law of the country. Who would say that a clergyman's crimes, should he commit theft or murder, were to be regarded as spiritual acts? The clergy are in these cases, and equally in all other civil relations, simply members of society, and as members of society they must be treated; they can claim no sort of exemption in virtue of their religious character. More than this, since the business of government is to maintain peace, it is the duty of the ruler to limit the number of clergymen in any part of the kingdom, should their growth appear likely to disturb the order and tranquillity of the State.

The power of the clergy is thus not only restricted to spiritual affairs; it can only be given effect to by Authority of the clergy. spiritual means. Temporal pains and penalties do not belong to the law of the Gospel, which indeed is not, properly speaking, a law at all but rather an injunction (*doctrina*); for ' it is not laid down that any man should in this world be compelled to its observance,' and coercive force is part of the definition of law. The priest may warn and threaten, but beyond this he has no competence. If a heretic become obnoxious to the civil law—if, in other words, his doctrine is dangerous to society—by that law he is to be tried: but of heresy, as such, there is but one judge, Jesus Christ, and his sentence is in the world to come; errors of opinion lie beyond the cognisance of any human judicature. Marsiglio has thus arrived at the fully matured principle of religious toleration, which modern writers are apt to vaunt as their own peculiar discovery, and which modern politicians are more ready to profess in theory than to carry into practice.

C. H.   C

It may be objected to Marsiglio's entire view of the spiritualty that he seems to leave out of account the existing constitution of the Church, that he seems to forget that custom had classified the priesthood in ascending orders of dignity and authority, each with its proper province of power and jurisdiction. But in truth, he maintains, this arranagement is destitute of any Scriptural warrant. In the New Testament *bishop* and *priest* are convertible designations of the same persons; and the Popedom, however convenient as symbolising the and of the Papacy. unity of the Church, is none the less a later institution of which the historical growth is clearly traceable. Saint Peter had no superiority over the other apostles; but even supposing he had, it is hazardous to assert that he communicated it to his successors in the Roman See, since we cannot say for certain that he himself ever visited, far less was Bishop of, Rome at all. The pre-eminence of the Bishop of Rome proceeds in fact not from Saint Peter's institution but from the connexion of the see with the capital of the Roman Empire. The supreme power in the Church is the Church itself, that is, a general council, formed of the clergy and laity alike, and convoked not by any pretended spiritual authority but by the source of all legislation and jurisdiction, the civil State. Thus constituted a general council may not only decide ecclesiastical questions but even excommunicate the temporal ruler and place his land under an interdict, just because it represents the authority of the universal Church and speaks the voice of the entire community both in its spiritual and temporal constituencies. That it has power over the Pope follows necessarily from the principles already laid down.

It is evident then that the Pope in his quality of Christian bishop can claim no right of supreme judgement in human things, even over the clergy. If he possess any such right it must have been conceded to him by human authority ; as a spiritual person he has absolutely none, and therefore properly he ought to possess none. When Christ gave to Saint Peter the keys of heaven and hell, this does not mean that the priesthood has the power by the sentence of excommunication to place a man under civil disabilities. The keys open and close the door of forgiveness, but forgiveness is the act of God, determined by the penitence of the sinner. Without these conditions the priestly absolution is of no avail. The turnkey, *claviger,* is not the judge. And as for excommunication, that power belongs, as we have seen, properly not to the clergy by themselves but to the community of Christians.

Marsiglio goes through the standard arguments in favour of the Papal assumptions and rejects them one after another, partly by his resolute insistence on a rational interpretation of the text of Scripture, partly by the essential distinction between the sacred calling of the priesthood and their extrinsic or worldly connexions. With his ideal of a Church in which these worldly ties have no existence, with his view of them as mere indications of the distance by which the actual Church is removed from primitive purity, there is no room for any talk of ecclesiastical privileges and exemptions. The sole privilege of the clergy is their spiritual character. Temporal sovereignty or jurisdiction is an accident of their civil position; and all inferences from the Bible which have been imagined to authorise it,—such as the famous argument of the 'two swords' (Luke xxii. 38) as typifying the double power, temporal as well as spiritual, of the clergy,— are incompatible not only with the conception of a Church, but also with the plain meaning of the texts from which they are deduced. *My kingdom is not of this world.*

It is not too much to say that we have here in the *Defensor Pacis* the whole essence of the political and religious theory which separates modern times from the Middle Ages. The significance of the protestant Reformation, putting theological details aside, lay in the substitution of a ministry serving the Church, the congregation of Christian men, for a hierarchical class. The significance of the later political revolution lay in the acceptance of the people as the source of government, as the sovereign power in the State. Both these ideas Marsiglio made his own. He had not only a glimpse of them as from afar off: he thought them out, defined them, stated them with the clearest precision, so that the modern constitutional statesman, the modern protestant, has nothing to alter in their principle, has only to develop them and fill in their outline. Marsiglio may be stigmatised as a *doctrinaire*, but he belongs to that rarest class of *doctrinaires* whom future ages may rightly look back upon as prophets.

There is no doubt a certain element in Marsiglio's speculations in which he shows himself entirely the

child of his age. This is when he approaches the
question whether the Church should hold any property.
As an ally of the Fraticelli he cannot but answer it
in the negative. The ministers of the Church should
be supported by those to whom they minister but
only in the necessaries of life; but 'no one of the
faithful is bound by Scripture to pay them the tenth
or any other part of his income.' The clergyman
might well supply his needs by other means, as by
handicraft, after the example of the apostles. But
now that the Church has been enriched by ample
endowments, the question arises, to whom do these
endowments belong? Granted that the clergy have
the use of them, who is the real owner? Marsiglio
replies that the property can only belong to the
person or persons who gave it, or to the State. Nor
can the clergyman claim the entire use of it: he is
the administrator of a trust; and what is left over
after his daily food and raiment are supplied, must
be distributed to the poor. In all this Marsiglio
is at one with his Franciscan friends; only what was
the premise of their argument, is the consequence of
his: his doctrine of 'evangelical poverty' flows by an
irresistible, if literalist, logic from the larger doctrine
of the spiritual character of the clergy. With Ockham
on the other hand it was a purely theological dispute,
almost a mere matter of partisanship, from which he
advanced to combat the general assumptions of the
Papacy.

Yet Ockham was by far the more practical speculator
than his swifter and more adventurous fellow-worker.
He was more sensible of the difficulty, of the almost

hopeless intricacy, of the problems that called for solution. As strenuous as any man in contesting the William of 'plenitude of power' arrogated for the Ockham. Papacy, he was unwilling to transfer it to any other person or to any body of persons. The Pope was no supreme autocrat; indeed the Emperor was within certain limitations his natural judge. But if, as Ockham maintained, the Pope was fallible, so also was a general council. He gives us his idea of how such an assembly should be constituted: it should be representative not only of the laity side by side with the clergy, but also both of men and women. But even this general council he would not entrust with the absolute, final decision in matters of faith. Any man, all men, may err; and Ockham is constrained in the last resort to find consolation in the Scriptural paradox which speaks of the truth vouchsafed to little children. He is certain that the faith must live, but cannot admit without qualification any of the suggested sureties for its maintenance. He is so embarrassed by the various alternatives that arise in his mind, so persuaded of the elements of truth that each contains in different degrees, that he seems unable to form any fixed resolution on the whole subject. Revelation of course cannot but be infallible, but he is not sure, at least he does not tell us his opinion, of the limits to which the name is to be restricted. 'Authority' was at all times an ambiguous word, and all we can conclude positively is that Ockham did not understand it as including the canon law or any part of the special Roman tradition.

Ockham liked to draw out his arguments by means

of a dialogue [1] or in the scholastic form of ' questions.'
The method allows him to throw out the most startling
suggestions, but at the same time saves him from the
necessity of giving his own private opinion on any
point. We are generally left to guess it from a
balance of more or less conflicting passages. Thus
it is hardly possible to arrive at a clear view of his
conception of the Empire and the Papacy, in themselves
and in their mutual relations. He hints that in a
certain state of society it might be better to have
several Popes and several sovereigns ; and although he
recognises in some sort the claims of the theoretical
universal Empire, there is an air of unreality about his
assertions which lets us see that he has not forgotten
his English birth and French training. No human
institution is absolute or final, and neither Pope nor
Emperor can claim exemption from the general law of
progress and adaptation. If however at the present
time, Ockham argues, the prerogative of the Empire
reaches over the entire world in its temporal relations,
this must of course exclude the Pope from all but
spiritual functions. Ockham has travelled by a different road to the same point as Marsiglio. Neither
really cares about the imperial idea : all that is of im-

---

[1] His chief political work, the *Dialogus*, which is not preserved,
or at least not printed, in its entirety, is nearly four times as long as
the *Defensor Pacis*, and occupies five hundred and sixty folio pages
in Goldast's edition. It was certainly not written as a single work,
and probably consists of three or more distinct treatises. I may notice
that almost every writer upon Ockham's views on Church politics has
drawn his materials chiefly from the popular *Dialogue between a Knight
and a Clerk*, the authorship of which Dr. Riezler has clearly proved not
to be his.

portance to them is to erect the State into an organic, consolidated force, independent of, and in its own province superior to, the spiritualty ; and this done, they circumscribe even the spiritual part of the Papal authority by making it in all respects subject to the general voice of Christendom. The Pope remains the exponent of the Church, but appeal is always open to the Church, to the whole society, itself. The chief difference in the results of the two theorists is that Marsiglio is certain, while Ockham hesitates, about the unerring sagacity of this final arbiter.

With all his vigour and independence Ockham as a political writer stands clearly on a lower level than his Italian fellow-worker. He had not that prescience of the new order for which the world was becoming ripe that raises Marsiglio above the whole rank of antagonists to the hierarchical policy of the Church in the Middle Ages. Ockham, like his successor Wycliffe, was immersed in the petty, or at best the transitory, interests of scholasticism. In theological doctrine Wycliffe may by some be considered to have done more signal service. But his thoughts and those of his fellows move within the confined limits of their own time. The political theory of Wycliffe, with all its nobility, rests upon as wilful, as preposterous, a treatment of the Bible as that of any of his hierarchical adversaries. Carried into practice by those who were not able to appreciate his refinements, it resolved itself into a species of socialism which was immediately seen to be subversive of the very existence of society. Marsiglio on the contrary is to a wonderful degree exempt from the trammels of tradition. Except when he urges the necessity of a return to evangelical poverty, or when he enlarges on the matters at issue between King Lewis and John the Twenty-second, we are hardly recalled to the age in which he lived. There can indeed be little doubt that he learned very much from Ockham in the years when they worked together at Paris; but the principles he then adopted he elaborated with far greater freedom than his friend. Ockham remains through all his writings first and foremost a scholastic theologian; Marsiglio ventures freely into the open field of political philosophy. Nor on the other hand can it be questioned that Ockham in his turn fell strongly under the influence of the Italian speculator. All his known works on ecclesiastical politics were produced at a later time than the *Defensor Pacis.* That work was written before Marsiglio took any active part against the Pope, while Ockham's works are the defence and justification of his share in that resistance. Thus while Marsiglio ran far ahead of his better-known contemporary, though he departed so much more widely from any previous theory of the relation of Church and State, Ockham's books are the later in point of time. In fact while the former quite overleaps the confines of the Middle Ages, Ockham preserves the orderly sequence and continuity of mediæval thought: and more than this, while Marsiglio in the daring of his speculation stands absolutely alone, Ockham, by virtue of his greater conformity to the spirit of his day,—not to speak of his eminence as a philosopher, unequalled among contemporaries and hardly surpassed by the great schoolmen of the generation before him,—handed down a light which was never suffered to be extinguished, and which served as a beacon to pioneers of reform like Wycliffe and Hus. In politics as well as in some points of doctrine, Ockham may be claimed as a precursor of the German Reformers of the sixteenth century; but Marsiglio hardly exercised any direct influence on later movements of thought. The principles which he brought into view had to be rediscovered, without even the knowledge that he had found them out beforehand, by the political philosophers of modern times.

Still it was with a true instinct that Gregory the Eleventh, in first taking cognisance of Wycliffe's views, averred that some of them contained the doctrine of the *Defensor Pacis*, 'doctrinam indoctam damnatæ memoriæ Marsilii de Padua.'[1] Wycliffe was seen to be the successor of Marsiglio.

---

[1] *Fasciculi Zizaniorum*, p. 243, ed. Shirley; Walsingham, *Historia Anglicana*, I. 346 ff., ed. Riley. With Marsiglio the bull couples the name of John of Jandun, who is stated to have been joint author of the *Defensor Pacis;* but as his share in the work is uncertain, I have not thought it worth while to distract the reader's attention by mentioning him in the text. My own conjecture is that John helped Marsiglio in the legal details of the treatise.

CHAPTER III.

THE POPES AT AVIGNON—THE PAPACY AND ENGLAND.

THE feeling which had been aroused against the pretension to contest temporal sovereigns made by Boniface the Eighth and John the Twenty-second, was not likely to subside so long as the Popes remained at Avignon. The site which Clement the Fifth had chosen for his residence brought the Papacy into a necessary connexion with France and with the French house now reigning at Naples, and thus with the Guelfic faction throughout Italy. The Pope became a partisan, and a French partisan. He might struggle against the overpowering influence of the French Crown; but if he had to contend with sovereigns like Philip the Fair or Philip of Valois he would generally struggle in vain. It was only during the interval between these Kings, when France was ruled by the three sons of Philip the Fair, that the Pope could venture upon independent action. Still, even if the Popes could at any time feel themselves free from the control of the French King, none the less was their policy guided by French interests. The college of cardinals became in effect a

Connexion of the Papacy with France.

French club; the policy of the Pope was, as a rule, the policy of the King of Naples, the King of Naples commonly the close ally of France.

Nor was the Papacy merely tending more and more to become a political institution; its spirit and whole manner of life was becoming secularised. Loss of character, No doubt there had usually been luxury enough and splendour enough when the Popes lived at Rome or in its neighbourhood; but at Avignon the spiritual character of the Papacy seemed in danger of being totally forgotten. John the Twenty-second had used his position mainly as a means of getting money and providing for his friends. His successor, Benedict the Twelfth, righteously broke the tradition; he set his face firmly against nepotism, the holding of benefices in plurality, and the like abuses; but this very fact made the cardinals all the more anxious to restore it. When Benedict died they elected a French courtier and statesman who took the name of Clement the Sixth, and Clement reproduced and perpetuated Clement VI. the system. His manners, and for that 1342-1352. matter his morals, were entirely those of a man of the world; and under his rule Avignon became more than ever notorious for its sensuality and splendour: it had the same sort of reputation as Paris had in the time of the Second Empire. The contradiction between the theory and the reality of the Holy See had never been so glaring since its rise to ascendency in the eleventh century: the 'Church' might now seem to be quite lost in the 'world,' and the Pope to be in effect no longer the spiritual head of Christendom, but the prince of a secular court.

It was thus also that his opponents treated him. Nothing can be more significant of the influence exerted by the controversial works of which we have spoken in

and prestige.

the preceding chapter, than the statement of a contemporary chronicler that Duke Albert of Austria in 1343, in refusing to allow the interdict of Pope Clement to be observed in his dominions, explained that the *Dialogus* of Ockham had been sent him by the Emperor Lewis ;—evidently this, he means, had supplied him with a knowledge of the true bearing of the facts. Nor is this an isolated example ; on all sides, excepting in France itself, we see signs of the irritation which the Papal policy excited. In 1338 at their memorable meeting at Rense the German electors unanimously declared that the title of him whom they chose as king was valid without the confirmation of the Pope, thus repudiating the specific claim from which Lewis's conflict with John the Twenty-second had arisen. Nor again was the feeling displayed confined to open political opponents. In this same year two cardinals arrived in England with a mission to effect a pacification between Edward the Third and Philip of Valois. They were at once seen to be French partisans, and the Archbishop of Canterbury himself preached against them. Just then too Edward was made Imperial Vicar by Lewis. Pope Benedict remonstrated in vain, and the appointment was only revoked when Lewis found it to his advantage to come to terms with France. Edward all the while was professing the utmost devotion to the Pope, but he calmly refused to accept his ruling in these affairs of State. Except in the conventional phraseology of the

correspondence there is hardly a pretence at regarding
the Papacy as a spiritual power: it was treated to all
intents and purposes simply as any other of the powers
of Europe, with interests of its own, just as England
or France might have its private, national interests.
The Popes had their victory over Lewis the Bavarian,
but the victory cost them a large part of the prestige
which was still left to them in the eyes of religious
men.

Meanwhile their absence from Italy, where they held,
it must be remembered, vast territorial dominions, left
Effect upon that country a prey to every sort of disorder,
Italy. petty despotisms rising into prominence in
the north, and the encroachments of the King of
Naples advancing upward from the south of the
peninsula. Rome itself was in a state of perpetual
anarchy through the feuds of the noble families of the
city and the lack of any firmly established government.
Yet the Roman revolution of 1347, the famous tri-
bunate of Rienzi, must not be confounded
Rienzi. with movements hostile to the Papacy, nor
must it be given more importance than it really
deserves. Rienzi (Cola the son of Lorenzo) took his
first steps towards obtaining the sovereignty of Rome
in union with the Papal legate, Raymond bishop of
Orvieto. The legate was no doubt his docile instrument; but still for most of the brief months in which
Rienzi ruled, he had the Church on his side. A man
of great eloquence and enthusiasm, of high-pitched and
often visionary ideas, he infused his own spirit into the
Roman people, and made them believe that the dreams
which he had called up out of old Roman history were

capable of realisation in the time of Rome's utter degradation. Such was the sway he held over them that the people were content to submit to an administration of justice far more severe, because far more equitable, than anything that had been known to them for centuries. But the city, it is evident enough, was not prepared for such a revolution as he carried out. It might prevail for a moment,—actually, it held its ground from May to December 1347;—but the causes which had so long made Rome a scene of tumult and anarchy could not be uprooted once for all. Rienzi himself was not fitted by nature for the calm continuous government of a State. He became vain-glorious, arrogant, egoistic : he ceased to believe in himself,— the most dangerous thing for a man who has raised himself to power ;—and thus at almost the first breath of opposition he fled from Rome, and hid himself among the Fraticelli on the border of Naples.

The choice of his retreat is significant, for we cannot but observe that a movement such as he led implied a necessary reflexion on the Popes whose departure from Rome had caused the disorders he sought to remedy : Rienzi was making reforms which it was their duty to have made. He condemned in indignant language their desertion of the holy city. Hence it was that he fell under the censure and malediction of Clement the Sixth as a usurper of the Papal rights. While professing and intending the utmost reverence for the Church, Rienzi was vigorous in attacking abuses in it as well as in the State. He desired to reform both. He was aware how far the Church of his day was separated from that of the apostles. Perhaps

already during his Roman ascendency he was imbued,
as we know he was afterwards, with the Franciscan
doctrine of evangelical poverty. We cannot help com-
paring him with that older Roman patriot, Arnold of
Brescia, who held and enforced the same views as to
poverty and primitive purity years before
Saint Francis was born, who made a revo-
1146.
lution in Rome not unlike Rienzi's, but who, unlike
Rienzi, fell a victim to a greater power than
himself and was condemned to death by the
1155.
Emperor Frederick Barbarossa.

Rienzi remained in obscurity for more than two
years. Then, in the summer of 1350, he went to
Prague to lay his case before the Emperor, now Charles
the Fourth, most ecclesiastical of princes, who would
have no dealings with him until he had made his peace
with the Pope. To Avignon therefore Rienzi proceeded, was tried by three cardinals, and—
the common penalty when a man was less
1352.
a criminal than a dangerous person to leave at large—
was condemned to imprisonment. But nothing can
show us more decisively how unreal was the cause of
his condemnation than the fact that in the very next
year he was sent back by the Pope, with the title of
senator, in company with the military cardinal legate
Albornoz, to set matters in order in Rome. He had
not been long there before a riot broke out, and the
fickle populace fell upon him and slew him.
October 8,
The tribuneship or senatorship of Rienzi left
1354.
no imitators: Rome, with or without a Pope in her
midst, went on as before; and no attempt was made
to restore the idea of a Republic until a century later,

and then the attempt was as futile as Rienzi's had been.

At the death of Clement the Sixth in December 1352 the college of cardinals was almost wholly French. He had himself promoted twenty-nine cardinals, and twenty-four of them were Frenchmen. The college before entering the conclave for the election of a new Pope passed two resolutions, one to prevent the enlargement of their number and thus to secure for themselves a permanent majority, the other establishing their right to one-half of the Papal revenue. Innocent VI., They then elected Stephen Aubert, a Limou-1352–1362. sin, who took the title of Innocent the Sixth. He immediately rescinded the act of the college to which as cardinal he had sworn a few days before. He set his face firmly against pluralities, non-residence, and similar abuses; nepotism was a licence which he only allowed to himself. He also tried to keep the vices and extravagance of the cardinals within bounds, and personally showed a good example in this respect. The success of his legate Albornoz in reducing the Papal dominions in Italy to comparative tranquillity might now appear to open the way for the Papal Court to return to Rome. But Innocent had no ambition to enter upon so dangerous an enterprise. While France was sinking into temporary insignificance, he still kept to the fixed policy of his predecessors; he held aloof from Edward the Third, and resolutely declined to promote a single English cardinal.

His successor William Grimoald, Urban the Fifth, was a Benedictine monk of high character. Frugal and austere in his own life, he did as much as any man

could to check the abuses which still reigned in the
Court at Avignon.   What he saved in display and
luxury he spent munificently in founding
and restoring monasteries ; he founded himself a college at Montpellier for the study of theology
and the canon law, and supported (we are told) no less
than a thousand scholars in different universities.   The
real earnestness of Urban's aims is proved by the fact
that he not merely promised, as several Popes before
him had done, to return to Rome, but actually did
return.   The city itself was too insecure
for a permanent residence, but Urban maintained himself not far off, at Montefiascone, for three
years.   The constant opposition however of his cardinals, who pined after the delights of Avignon, added
to the unruly state of the country which Albornoz had
only been able for a time to appease, compelled the Pope at last to go back to Avignon, where in a few months he died.   He was followed
by Gregory the Eleventh, a nephew of Clement the
Sixth, whom his uncle had made a cardinal
at the age of seventeen or eighteen, and had
carefully educated in the professional studies of theology and canon law.   Gregory, though a man of great
ability, was continually foiled by the political difficulties against which he had to contend.   In France
itself, despite the treaty of Brétigny, there was chronic
war on a small but not less exasperating scale, while
in Italy the rise of the Visconti to ascendency threatened to destroy once for all the territorial position of
the Papacy there.   It was this latter cause which induced the Pope to follow Urban's example and return

Urban V., 1362.

1367.

December 1370.

Gregory XI.

to Rome. He reached the city in January 1377, and like Urban, there is little doubt, would have abandoned the undertaking had he not been surprised by death— he was only forty-seven—in the spring of the following year. With Gregory ends the inglorious line of the Avignonese Popes; his pontificate is followed by the humiliation of the long schism which distracted the allegiance of Europe for more than a generation.

While the Popes were mainly occupied with political affairs, and while the demoralisation in high places was Religious penetrating every rank in the Church, the disorder. religious disorder of the time manifested itself in various and incongruous forms. The laity sank into an easy-going secularism, only to be broken by occasional outbursts of fanatical enthusiasm. Thrice in the first half of the fourteenth century Italy was disquieted by the appearance of crowds of ' Flagellants,' wild people who expiated their sins by unremitting 1348-9. terrible scourgings : the third time, during the panic of the black death, the rage spread over Western Europe ; a visitation of this sort was never unattended with movements of religious excitement. In England indeed the Flagellants hardly made any stir ; in France the King and the University of Paris forbade and condemned their practices : but in Germany and the Low Countries their fanaticism was unrestricted and beyond control. They heralded the end of the world, plainly foreshown (it was held) by the universal pestilence. Superstitious beliefs of different kinds seem now to grow in prevalence. The chronicles are full of records of persons ' possessed,' and of their fearful deaths. Prophecy is revived and

visionary preachers acquire a strange sway over the
people, especially of Italy, and even over the less
excitable Popes. Some, like the friar John de Roche-
taillade, were quietly suppressed by life-long imprisonment; but others, the two prophetesses, Saint Bridget
of Sweden and Saint Catharine of Siena, enthusiasts
with the purest aims but of highly hysterical temperament, had no little influence in arousing among
the Italians a sense of the necessity that society should
reform itself, as well as in urging the Popes to take
up their residence once more at Rome. The very extravagance of these religious movements is but a new
evidence that the life of the Church was deranged and
needed to be disciplined by more Christian rulers than
those it then possessed. There was not one of these
preachers or prophets who did not couple, with his
visions of the future, denunciations, as severe as they
were true, of the vices of the Papal government. But
the first declared resistance to it on a large scale of
which we have to speak started not from the moral so
much as from the political difficulties which it was felt
to involve.

France in the days of Boniface the Eighth, Germany
under John the Twenty-second, had each shown how
a national feeling must perforce rise into existence
against the aggression of the Papacy. England, as
yet peculiarly free from heresy, and liberal above other
countries in its gifts to the Papal treasury, was now
to take up the cause which France had no longer any
reason for maintaining, and which Germany had given
over in despair. And England, thanks partly to the

submission of King John, was treated by the Popes in a more masterful way than other countries.[1] During the reign of Edward the Second Papal provisions and reservations,—that is, in most cases, the appointment by the Pope to a benefice during the lifetime of the incumbent,—were multiplied to an extent previously unknown. Appeals to the Papal Court and applications for dispensations and other privileges from it were more and more felt as a national grievance. The annual tribute pressed the more hardly as the land was drained of its resources by the exhausting succession of wars with France. Against each of these practices Edward the Third took repeated and resolute action. When in

Provisions. 1343 Clement the Sixth 'provided' two cardinals to English benefices, the King expelled their proctors (who had come over to take possession) from the kingdom, and wrote a letter of serious expostulation to the Pope. But the effect of such remonstrances was generally lost, because the King was not disinclined to avail himself of the Pope's mediation for the purpose of appointing men whom he himself desired to promote. At last in 1351 the statute of Provisors condemned to imprisonment all who should receive Papal provision, at the same time ingeniously transferring the patronage of such benefices to the King. The Pope however still retained his right to appoint to sees left vacant by translation,

---

[1] See on this whole subject Bishop Stubbs's *Constitutional History of England*, 3, ch. xix. : 'England seems to have been the great harvestfield of imposition.' Compare also Mr. Hunt's volume on *The English Church in the Middle Ages*, in the present series, which has appeared since this work was written.

that is, by the removal of a bishop from one see to another; and it is a sufficient proof that the Statute of Provisors had not afforded the necessary safeguard against the abuses at which it was aimed, that a congress had to be arranged in 1374 to reopen the whole question.[1]

The opportunity for escaping the jurisdiction of the royal courts by an appeal to Rome was not unnatu-

Appeals.

rally regarded as an injury to the rights of the King of England. In 1358, when the Bishop of Ely carried an appeal to the Pope, and obtained the excommunication of some members of the royal Council, the King imprisoned the envoys from the Papal Court, had them tried by his justices, and finally put to death. But it is certain that since the death of Henry the Third appeals of an important character had become greatly reduced in number. The ordinance of 1353 'against annullers of judgement in the King's courts' forbade under stringent penalties the prosecution in foreign courts of suits cognisable by the law of England. In 1365 a statute was passed which expressly directed the prohibition against suitors in the Papal Court; and finally the great statute of Præmunire in 1393 declared that any one who should obtain bulls or other instruments from Rome was liable to forfeiture. The Popes in vain attempted to obtain the repeal of this statute, and from the date of its enactment appeals to Rome became less and less frequent. At the same time the spirit of it was evaded by the continued permission of the practice of dispensations. Instead of cases being heard by

[1] See below, pp. 75 f.

the Pope in person, they were now brought before
judges whom he commissioned to act for him in England; and thus in reality the foreign jurisdiction remained, though it was now exercised on English soil.
The King had still the power to prohibit such acts,
but he found it convenient to waive it.

The third cause of discontent against the Roman
Court to which we have referred arose from the obligation of paying an annual tribute of a thousand
marks to the Pope. On financial grounds,
especially during the French war, this debt was felt
to be burthensome; it had already fallen into arrear
since 1333. Still if this payment was a legal due, the
fact of its inconvenience would furnish no argument
against its payment. It was however regarded as an
imposition resting upon a personal act of King John,
unauthorised by and thoroughly dishonourable to the
English nation; and this is the reason why it not merely
fell into arrear but was at length repudiated. We may
be inclined to dispute the morality of this repudiation,
which was sanctioned in 1366; but the truth is that
parliamentary institutions had by that time become so
necessary a part of our governmental machinery that
men were hardly able to go behind them and conceive
of a time when the King could constitutionally act
without them. Even had this not been the case, the
objection to recognise what this payment implied,
namely, the feudal dependence of the English Crown
upon the Roman See, at a time when the Pope was
understood to be the declared ally of France, is an
objection clearly intelligible, if not defensible, on
grounds of genuine national sentiment. For our

The tribute. (side note)

present purpose the repudiation of the tribute is of
interest since it gave, so far as is known, the first
opportunity to Wycliffe for appearing as the supporter of the parliamentary contention against the
Roman supremacy. It is worthy of notice that in
1374, when the Pope repeated his claim for the
tribute and demanded that the King should levy a
talliage to support him in his contest with the Florentines, while the churchmen present in a Great
Council refused to deny the Pope's right, the Provincial of the Dominican order asked to be excused
replying, but another friar John Mardesley flatly
denied all temporal power to the Papacy, and the
secular lords, seemingly with one consent, maintained that King John had no right whatever to
yield his realm to the Pope and that the grant was
totally illegal.[1]

Besides the tribute, the Roman Church drew an
income from England from three distinct sources:
Papal income first, there was the ancient Romescot or
from England. Peter's pence, which had long been com-
muted for about £200; secondly, there were fees for
bulls and dispensations, and on promotion to bishop-
ricks and other benefices; and thirdly, voluntary
offerings. It was not so much the sums that were
exacted as the manner of their exaction that raised
discontent. The collector appointed by the Pope
carried out his duties usually in such a way as to
make him highly unpopular both with the clergy and
the laity. Travelling through the country in great

---

[1] An account of these curious proceedings will be found in the
continuation of the *Eulogium Historiarum*, 3. 337 ff.

state and with a numerous retinue, his attitude was
apt to be imperious, and the offerings demanded by
him could hardly be described as voluntary. It was
complained by the Commons of the Good Parliament
that the collector's emissaries acted as spies, noting
vacancies—no doubt both present and prospective
vacancies—in benefices, with a view to the exercise of
patronage by the Pope.[1] Besides this, the very position of the collector in the kingdom was felt as an
intrusion, and an oath had to be framed to bind him
to do nothing against the King's majesty or the law of
the realm. Probably indeed in the latter part of the
fourteenth century the Papal collector was not so important a person as he had been in earlier times; yet
the feeling against him combined with a general irritation at the conduct of the Papacy, and like the question
of the tribute it furnished Wycliffe with an argument
against the secularised condition of the Church which
was accepted as just by a very considerable party among
the laity, and not the laity only, of England.

For the feeling of discontent spread itself in various
ways, and found expression in various forms. The
State of the risk that Church matters should enter into
English clergy. common party politics had now become
a reality. The high ecclesiastics saw that their
interests were to a great extent bound up with those
of the Pope, to whom many of them owed their appointment; and against them there rose up a powerful party among the nobility, who had no doubt views
of their own as to the proper persons to whom the

[1] Forty-fifth petition of Parliament of 1376, in the *Rotuli Parlia-
mentorum*, 2. 33S.

vast ecclesiastical revenues should be transferred. The
desire of plunder is a frequent element in reforming
policy; and in the days of Richard the Second a party
of the nobles, equally with the socialistic rebels of 1381,
though they started from entirely opposed principles,
tended towards schemes of spoliation. At the same
time the fact that a majority of the bishops generally
belonged to noble English families prevented the oc-
currence of more than temporary conflicts with the
secular nobility. Further, if they were divided among
themselves, much more were the inferior clergy. The
ordinary parish priest, the secular clergy at large, had
interests which placed them in direct and continual
conflict with the mendicant orders, and the mendicant
orders had a standing feud with the monks. The old
dispute about the necessity of the observance of poverty
was by no means forgotten, and every now and then
broke forth into violent controversy.

In 1356 Richard FitzRalph, Archbishop of Armagh, found such a controversy raging in London,
Friars and
Possessioners. and preached strongly against the Franciscan
tenets. The result was that by the influ-
ence of his opponents he was cited to Avignon; there
in November 1357 he made his defence in a sermon
which is still preserved and which throws a clear light
on the causes of the widespread animosity that existed
against the friars.[1] The Archbishop goes to the root
of the matter, and assails the principle of begging—
except for sheer need—as unauthorised by the example

---

[1] It is entitled *Defensorium Curatorum*, and has been several times
printed, *e.g.* in Edward Browne's Appendix to Gratius' *Fasciculus
Rerum expetendarum et fugiendarum*, pp. 466–486.

of Christ, and therefore, since this is the pattern laid
down by Saint Francis, unauthorised by the founder of
the order. His practical charges, however much ex-
aggerated we may hold them, are of particular interest.
The friars, he says, departed from the rules of their
profession in greed for increased power and influence.
They interfered with the legitimate authority of the
parish clergyman by taking upon themselves to hear
confessions. True, this privilege was once conceded
to them by Alexander the Fourth; but subsequent decrees had modified it so as not to impair the rights of
the parish priest: yet in spite of this the friars had
gradually gained an ascendency over the minds of the
people, and thus not merely done wrong to the parson
but diverted into the funds of their order the offerings
which should have been employed for the benefit of
the parish. Another charge made by FitzRalph is
that the friars encroached upon the rights of parents,
making use of the confessional to get hold of their
children and induce them to enter their convents, to
become in due time friars themselves. Hence, the
Archbishop states, the University of Oxford had fallen
to one-fifth of its former numbers: parents were unwilling to send their sons thither, and preferred to
bring them up as farmers, so that the ministry of the
Church failed of its natural supply.

It was the arguments of FitzRalph that furnished a
model to Wycliffe when at a late period in his career
he came to take up arms against the friars: Fitz-
Ralph was also the chief source of some of Wycliffe's
most characteristic views. Here however we only
notice his polemic as an illustration of the hostility

which existed between different sections of the Church.
No reader of contemporary chronicles written by
monks or by friars is ignorant of the strong motives
of interest and partisanship that held them asunder,
or of the strong expression which their animosity
took. While thus the jealous opposition of seculars,
friars, and monks, happily prevented the formation of
a single Church party with anti-national views,—a
danger which had arisen in earlier centuries of the
Middle Ages,—at the same time it helped to keep
alive the popular notion that the Church was in an
evil state. The prevalence of pluralities and non-
residence encouraged this idea; and it is probably not
too much to say that in the latter part of the fourteenth century there were few persons in England
(whose interests were not directly connected with
them) who were not sensible of the abuses under
which religion was labouring and of the necessity of
some sort of reform.

CHAPTER IV.

THE EARLY LIFE OF JOHN WYCLIFFE.

THERE are few medieval writers about whose early life we are at all satisfactorily informed. The most tangible facts about them commonly rest upon later tradition, and the contemporary data are as a rule so fragmentary that without fuller knowledge than we possess it is hopeless to reconcile their apparent contradictions. To no biography are these remarks more applicable than to that of John Wycliffe. Every fact in his early history has been the subject of lively controversy; and while in the present work results should be stated rather than processes, it will be impossible to avoid reference to the doubts which still hang over some of the critical points in his career.

For Wycliffe's birthplace, beyond Walsingham's statement that he was a northerner, our sole authority is John
Wycliffe's birth and family. Leland, who travelled through England in the search for historical materials in the latter part of the reign of Henry the Eighth. Leland tells us in one place that Wycliffe derived his origin from the village of Wycliffe-on-Tees, a name familiar to readers of *Marmion;* elsewhere he notices that

he was born at Ipreswel (evidently the place now
called Hipswell), a mile from Richmond in Yorkshire.
The two passages are of course easily reconcilable : one
indicates the family from which he sprang, the other
the village where he was actually born ; and there is
now no further difficulty about the matter, though all
his biographers have been misled by a misprint in the
edition of Leland into seeking after an imaginary village called Spreswell. The date of Wycliffe's birth is
entirely unknown. As he died of paralysis in 1384,
it has been argued that he must have been advanced
in years, so that it is unlikely that he was born much
after 1320.

After the practice of those days he no doubt came
up to Oxford quite young. The objection that the dan-
Education at   ger of the roads would preclude a boy from
Oxford.   making so long a journey is not only raised in
ignorance of the organisation of ' bringers of scholars '
and common carriers which was employed for this
particular purpose, but is also contradicted by the fact
of numerous pupils being sent to Oxford at a very
early age from all parts of England, in the Middle
Ages. Considering that, with an academical population of a good many thousands, only five small colleges
then existed, the probability would be that Wycliffe was
not attached to any college, were it not the case that
a specially northern college existed in the foundation
of the Balliols of Barnard Castle, not many miles
from his home, that several indications are found of a
connexion between his family and that college, and
above all that John Wycliffe himself subsequently
became Master of Balliol, an office which by statute

could only be given to a Fellow of the house. There is therefore no reason for disturbing the generally accepted view that it was here that he received his university education, though at the same time it is possible that he previously went through a rudimentary 'grammar' course, such as, in the dearth of local schools, was very commonly pursued at Oxford.

The studies required for the degree of Bachelor of Arts can only be gathered imperfectly from detached notices. The old distinction of the seven liberal arts, the *trivium* belonging to the undergraduate course, and the *quadrivium* being preliminary to the degree of Master, had long been obsolete, though the names lingered on. The immense expansion of philosophical interest consequent on the translation of the works of Aristotle in the twelfth and thirteenth centuries, before which time only some of his logical treatises had been known to Western Christendom, had in fact rendered the old classification quite inadequate. But the system which took its place is obscure. 'While grammar and logic were invariably studied before determination,' the last exercise before proceeding to the degree of Bachelor of Arts, ' and music, geometry, astronomy, and moral philosophy, after determination ; there was no fixed rule of general obligation as to the time at which rhetoric, arithmetic, and natural and metaphysical philosophy should be studied. Priscian, Donatus, and Terence were the authors most frequently read in the schools of grammar ; Porphyry, Boethius, Aristotle, and Petrus Hispanus, in those of logic ; and Aristotle

Studies.

again in those of the three philosophies.'[1] It is almost unnecessary to add that in Wycliffe's time Greek was unknown as a subject of study in Oxford. After about four years the scholar would 'determine,' at the age perhaps of seventeen or eighteen; three years of further study would enable him to 'incept,' in other words, to become a Master of Arts. Beyond this stage no Fellow of Balliol could proceed, since in 1325 the College had ordered, by a deed to which Richard FitzRalph was one of the signatories, that its Fellows should apply themselves exclusively to the liberal arts. The study of theology was thus prohibited to them, at least so far as it led to a degree in that faculty. In 1340 however a new endowment established six theological fellowships, the holders of which were bound to incept in divinity within thirteen years.

Under these conditions probably Wycliffe resided at Balliol until he was elected Master, some time after
Official career.　1356, but not later than 1360. A difficulty has indeed arisen from the fact that a certain John Wycliffe was Fellow of Merton in 1356. It is clear from the precision of the notice in the Merton records, that this Fellow was believed to be the reformer, by those who ought to have known, not many years after his death: at the same time there is a preponderance of evidence to show that he was confounded with a namesake. At least, as we have said, Wycliffe must have been a Fellow of Balliol at the time of his election as Master. So soon as 1361

[1] H. C. Maxwell Lyte, *History of the University of Oxford*, 206 f.

he accepted a college living, that of Fillingham in Lincolnshire, and probably left Oxford for some time. In 1363 however he was back again, this time resident in Queen's College, a fact which is explained by the practice of letting rooms not required by the college to other members of the University. At Queen's Wycliffe appears to have lived for part at least of the years 1363–5. In 1368 he obtained from the Bishop of Lincoln leave of absence from his benefice for the term of two years, in order to ' devote himself to the study of letters at Oxford ; ' but being presented almost immediately to the living of Ludgarshall in Buckinghamshire, he was probably able to combine his parochial duties with a frequent residence at Oxford, the distance being not more than some fifteen miles. Plainly his interests were more closely connected with his University than with his parish ; and if, as is generally believed, he was now engaged in the course of study required for a degree in theology, it was necessary for him to spend much of his time at Oxford.

But already Wycliffe had become an influential person not only at Oxford but at the royal Court. We have already noticed that in 1366 Parlia-

Connexion with the Court.

ment refused to pay tribute to the Pope. Whether Wycliffe had anything to do with counselling this policy is unknown ; but at least his advocacy was employed to defend it. A certain monk, it appears, had protested against the action of Parliament, and Wycliffe was called upon to reply. The tenour of the document which he produced [1] is decidedly of an

---

[1] *Determinatio quædam de dominio*, printed by John Lewis, *Life of Wiclif*, Appendix 30.

C. H.   E

official character. ' As,' he says, ' I am the King's chaplain (*peculiaris regis clericus talis qualis*) I willingly take upon myself the task of making answer.' Besides his own arguments, which are chiefly devoted to the maintenance of the view that the civil State has the power of depriving the Church of its possessions in case of need, Wycliffe gives an account of the speeches made by seven lords ' in a certain council' against the payment of the tribute. This has been some-times regarded as a genuine Parliamentary report; but some remarkable coincidences with Wycliffe's special political views, not to speak of the way in which each speaker is made to keep to an entirely distinct line of argument, show that whatever their foundation, the form in which the speeches are de-veloped is Wycliffe's own.

In this light the tract is of great interest as affording the first glimpse we have into his opinions on the general question of the relation of the civil State towards the Church. The second lord, for instance, argues that 'no tribute or rent should be granted save to those who are capable,' and therefore not to the Pope : ' for the Pope ought above all to be a follower of Christ, but Christ would not be a pro-prietor of civil lordship, and so neither should the Pope.' This is Wycliffe's doctrine of evangelical poverty. The third lord maintains that the Pope as ' the servant of the servants of God ' (in allusion to the formal heading of Papal documents) ought only to receive taxes in return for service (*ministerium*) rendered; but since he does nothing to benefit our kingdom, but on the contrary helps our enemies, we

ought to withhold the payment. Here again is
Wycliffe's position that 'lordship' involves the reci-
procal relation of 'service.' The fourth lord argues
that the Papal claim to be lord-in-chief of Church
property is prejudicial to the King's rights, since on
this showing one-third of the land of England must
be outside the King's lordship : but there cannot be
two lords of the same territory, so that only one of the
two can be truly lord-in-chief; and this lord-in-chief
must be the King. A similar statement as to the
amount of ecclesiastical property in England (except
that it is now reduced to one-fourth) appears later on
in Wycliffe's treatise *De Ecclesia* (ch. xv.) with the
same inference as to its bearing on the royal prerogative. The fourth lord proceeds to say that, since
the Pope in these respects plainly 'holds' of the
King, he ought to do homage and service for his
tenancy ; which as he omits, he forfeits all rights,
and the obligation of paying tribute ceases. The
fifth lord maintains that King John's surrender as the
price of his absolution and of the relaxation of the
interdict was in itself simoniacal, and therefore void ;
an argument much more likely to occur to a theologian than to a layman. We give these examples
of the lords' speeches, partly in order to show that,
in the shape in which we have them, they are not
speeches actually made by the advocates of King
Edward's policy, but rather represent the arguments
which appealed to Wycliffe himself as appropriate to
the occasion ; and partly to introduce the reader to a
style of reasoning which forms a highly characteristic
element in Wycliffe's treatment of Church politics.

Just before this first action of Wycliffe's in regard to public affairs, he had received, according to the view Supposed post at Oxford. now generally accepted, the office of Warden of Canterbury Hall in Oxford,[1] a foundation the site of which is still marked by the Canterbury quadrangle of Christ Church. This Hall had been established a few years earlier by Simon Islip, archbishop of Canterbury, as a mixed foundation of monks and secular clergymen ; in December 1365 he removed the regulars and appointed seculars in their place, with Wycliffe at their head. Obviously, as indeed one might have foretold from the beginning, the association of clerks in many ways so opposed was not a successful arrangement ; and we can hardly doubt that the change made by the Archbishop was determined by some definite outbreak of hostility between the rival elements in the Hall. At the same time it could scarcely be expected that the monks of Christ Church, Canterbury, for whom it had been in part designed, would bear the loss of their privilege patiently. So when Islip

---

[1] In a popular work like this I give the accepted statement. But I am bound to add that I am by no means convinced of its truth. Archbishop Islip was at the time he nominated the Warden, lying paralysed at Mayfield in Sussex, and the vicar of Mayfield was a John Wycliffe, who had in all probability been a Fellow of Merton College —Islip's own college—and had been presented to his living by the Archbishop. Combining these facts I cannot but believe that it was this Wycliffe who was made Warden of Canterbury Hall. His Wardenship was of short duration ; it ended in a scandal ; and it was almost inevitable that, wilfully or not, the identity of name should cause this scandal to be used against the reformer. Wycliffe's own allusion to the subject (*De Eccl.*, cap. xvi. pp. 370 f.) need not mean more than that the case occurred within the knowledge of those whom he was addressing, not necessarily that it related to himself personally.

died, and the Benedictine Simon Langham became archbishop in his room, Wycliffe was naturally enough ousted, and with him all his secular fellows. It was seen that the foundation could only consist satisfactorily of one of the two classes, and the monks were now in favour. Perhaps both the appointment and the removal of Wycliffe were somewhat high-handed actions, but it is hard to to say whether either Archbishop overstepped his lawful powers, except in omitting to seek the royal confirmation for his appointment.

Wycliffe and his friends appealed to Rome, but their proctor on more than one occasion failed to appear before the Court, in spite of due summons. Contumacy like this was fatal to a suit, but the Papal Court seems to have given an honest judgement against Wycliffe, since there could be no manner of doubt that the original scheme of foundation expressly considered the interests of the monks, and these interests had been set at nought by Islip's subsequent change. Granted that the Hall, if it was to prosper, must consist only of monks or of seculars, the former might fairly possess the prior claim. The Papal decision was given on the 11th May 1370; it was confirmed by the King on the 8th April 1372. The dates are of importance because it has lately been pretended that Wycliffe only turned to politics when his deprivation from the Wardenship at Canterbury Hall had discredited him at Oxford; whereas it is undisputed that his political activity began in 1366, and at the same time his Latin works prove that from this time onwards he was as regularly engaged in teaching at Oxford as his parish duties allowed him to be. If any blame attaches to any one in the affair of Canterbury Hall, it must be to Archbishop Islip. All the other features of the dispute are common to the endless rivalry between monk and secular which we encounter continually in the Middle Ages. The question throughout is one of party rather than one of right and wrong.

If this series of transactions really refers to Wycliffe the reformer and not to a namesake, we derive from it one more fact in his academical advancement, namely, that by the time of his appeal to Urban the Fifth he was a Bachelor of Divinity. That in 1374 he was a Doctor is known positively from the letters patent nominating him to be a member of the royal commission to confer with the Papal representatives at Bruges on the question of 'provisions;' but how much earlier he proceeded to that degree there is at present no means of ascertaining. This date however is of peculiar importance, since it has been uniformly stated that it was first after his admission to the degree of Doctor that Wycliffe fell into erroneous views in matters of theology. Considering the time of life at which he had now arrived it is perhaps allowable to conjecture that the date was prior to 1370. Various attempts have been made to fix this supposed turning-point in Wycliffe's career more closely.[1] It was asserted in his

1367-8.

First departure from orthodoxy.

---

[1] Shirley's argument for a much earlier date, derived from a statement of Wycliffe's in his *Determinatio contra Kylingham* (printed in the appendix to the *Fasciculi Zizaniorum*, p. 456), appears to rest upon a forced interpretation of that passage.

own lifetime that his deprivation of the Wardenship of Canterbury Hall led him to oppose the monastic system. Another early but unsupported tradition declared that disappointment at not being promoted to the bishoprick of Worcester—either in 1363 or 1368—was the cause of his attack upon Church endowments. But even if the facts be so, it is hopeless to argue about motives. A personal element is too often present in the actions of the best men ; but we have no right to seek it in what may be after all merely the scandal current among their detractors. Besides, when a man comes into collision with a system, it is perfectly possible for him thus to become alive to defects in that system which he had previously accepted without suspicion as part of the established order of things, without this change of view being at all associated with personal feelings of jealousy or disappointment. In Wycliffe's own case it is sufficient to observe that until in 1381 he extended his attack to the doctrine of transubstantiation he was treated with the greatest respect by opponents. In his controversy with Cuningham, for instance, both combatants hit hard ; but the blows are given with the accustomed weapons of ·mediæval disputation. There is a mixture of respectful criticism and of mild banter which shows us that we are reading simply a scholastic controversy between friends. Wycliffe's bitterest opponents, contemporary and later, are unanimous in their testimony to the high, if not the unique, position which he occupied in the Oxford schools ; and it is remarkable that when in 1377 Pope Gregory the Eleventh issued five bulls against sundry opinions attributed to him, three of these addressed to the

Archbishop of Canterbury and the Bishop of London
make no mention of heresy, a word which only occurs
in the bulls sent to the King and to the University of
Oxford. The distinction may appear trivial; but,
remembering the care with which Papal documents
were drawn up, it seems lawful to infer that the Pope
did not then feel justified in bringing a charge of heretical depravity against Wycliffe under a strictly ecclesiastical cognisance.

The difficulty which exists in attempting to fix
accurately the steps by which he was led into heretical opinions has not yet been removed by
any positive evidence in his Latin writings.

Stages in his opinions.

When we consider that in all probability the whole
mass of his English works, including the two translations of the Bible of which he was in part the author,
are crowded into the last six or eight years of his life,
we cannot say with certainty that his Latin writings,
which are in the main earlier than his English ones,
must necessarily have occupied more than a like number of years. All that can be safely affirmed is that
a certain number of works of a distinctly scholastic
character, and with no features of individuality to
separate them from others of their class, belong to
an earlier date, let us say, than his admission to the
degree of Doctor of Divinity, an event which we have
placed approximately in 1370. From this time onwards he devoted himself to expanding and illustrat-
ing the views which he had doubtless already delivered
in academical 'determinations' and lectures. Of such
a development we have a clear instance in the relation
subsisting between the tract concerning the Papal

tribute in 1366 and his great work *On Civil Lord-ship*, of which we can only say positively that it was written previously to 1377. The career of Wycliffe as an ecclesiastical politician runs evidently straight on from 1366; though his important writings on subjects involved in his political position are apparently some years later. It is clear that the Papal schism of 1378 was a determining force in the current of Wycliffe's speculation on the problem of Church and State; but there is no sort of break in its course. Gradually unfolding his views and gradually seeking to find his way to the bottom of the points at issue, he arrived at the double conclusion that the influence of the priesthood, as such, must be counterworked by the instruction of the laity in religious matters in their mother-tongue, and that the superstitious power (as he conceived it) attaching to the office of the priest rested upon the doctrine of transubstantiation, a doctrine which Wycliffe came to believe was not founded on the authority of Holy Scripture. This last stage in his life is definitely dated in the spring of 1381; while his organisation of a system for English religious teaching can hardly have been begun earlier than the condemnation of his views by the Pope in 1377. Thus from being a mere scholastic theologian Wycliffe came into conflict with the ruling forces in the Church first through his views as to the relation between Church and State, and secondly through his denial of what had been for some centuries a cardinal doctrine of Western Christianity.

To this digression from the main course of Wycliffe's biography we may add one remark which is the more needful since it relates to a question which has been often agitated on insufficient knowledge: during all Wycliffe's earlier career he had professed nothing but respectful admiration for the mendicant orders; in attacking Church endowments he had naturally opposed the monks, the 'possessioners,' as well as the rich secular clergy, but the friars remained free from his assault; it is only in the last stage of his career that his polemic is directed, and now directed specially, against the friars. In other words the views which, perhaps in oral lectures, perhaps in written treatises, he had learned from Richard FitzRalph, Archbishop of Armagh (who had been Vice-Chancellor of the University of Oxford about 1333), Wycliffe had at first applied only to the elaboration of his doctrine of *dominium* or 'lordship;' he had been content to combine them with the Franciscan position, which he had read in Ockham, of the necessity of evangelical poverty. In later years, while retaining his belief in this obligation, he accepted FitzRalph's attitude of uncompromising hostility to the mendicant orders. The seeming paradox of opposing the friars and yet upholding their specific tenet may be explained by the distance at which the friars of Wycliffe's day stood from the manner of life enjoined by their founders. At the same time it can hardly be questioned that the alliance which existed between the orders and the Papacy was not without influence in deciding Wycliffe's opposition to them.

Friendly relations with the friars.

CHAPTER V.

WYCLIFFE AND ENGLISH POLITICS.

WE now return to the time in Wycliffe's life in which
as Doctor of Divinity he was actively engaged in work
at Oxford, holding at the same time his living of
Ludgarshall and a position of influence—probably he
was still chaplain—at the Court. Of the favour in
which he stood we have two proofs, both in the year
1374. First in April he was nominated by the Crown
(in the minority of the patron of the living) to the
rectory of Lutterworth in Leicestershire. Next in
July he was appointed one of the royal ambassadors to confer with the Papal representatives at Bruges; his name stands second
on the commission, next after that of the Bishop of
Bangor; and the dignity of his office is shown by
the fact that he received payment at the noble rate (according to the then current value of money) of twenty
shillings a-day. The negotiations were concerned with
the old question of the Pope's right to interfere with
Church-appointments in England, but the results were,
as might be expected, practically illusory. Temporary
concessions were made both on the part of the Pope
and of the King, but they were such as might seem

*Wycliffe Royal
Commissioner
at Bruges.*

rather to establish than to impair the former's claim. It is however possible that some further points of agreement were arrived at, as a consequence of the congress, though not actually decided at that time; since certain articles which were laid before Parliament in February 1377, contain concessions which were stated to have been made by the Pope, though not committed to writing. Still, as we have before said, it was rather for the King's interest to make use of the Pope's pretension for the benefit of his own candidates than to surrender it in obedience to the national complaints. A system of collusion kept the system of provisions alive long after it was statutorily condemned.

The commissioners at Bruges had their reward: the chief, Bishop Gilbert, was translated to the more valuable see of Hereford; Wycliffe was given a prebend in the collegiate church of Westbury, which he soon resigned, possibly from some scruple about the tenure of benefices in plurality. Henceforward he was plain rector of Lutterworth and resided often at his living, though it is also certain that he gave up neither his occupation as a theological teacher at Oxford nor as an influential person in London, where he used to preach, and is admitted even by his enemies to have made a strong impression both upon nobles and citizens. *Association with John of Gaunt.* Whether or not it was through John of Gaunt that he first came into notice at Court, it was manifestly through this connexion that he continued to be employed as the Duke's agent in what many people regarded as mere partisan work. The problem of Church and State in John of Gaunt's mind

assumed the simple form, how best to plunder the rich
ecclesiastics for his own ends : Wycliffe's position in
the matter was that endowments were an innovation,
and a hindrance to the proper spiritual purpose of the
Church. The ideas of the two converged only in their
common dislike of the endowed classes whether of
priests or monks. Wycliffe possibly did not see clearly
how far his protector aimed ; he was content to be
made use of, with his mind too full of his own honest
desire for the purification of the Church, for him to be
able to perceive that the alliance into which he had
entered was very naturally liable to be misunderstood.
He was regarded as the Duke's tool, and was attacked
as such.

In February 1377 he was summoned to appear
before Convocation in London to answer sundry charges
Summons at
St. Paul's. of erroneous teaching. What these charges
were is not known, but there can be little
doubt that they related to his views on the subject of
the possessions of the Church and to the limitation
which he sought to impose upon the power of excommunication. His appearance in Saint Paul's Cathedral
of itself shows us the character which the case bore.
He was accompanied by the Duke of Lancaster and by
the Marshal of England, the same Lord Percy who was
a few months later raised to the earldom of Northum-
berland. Four Doctors of Divinity belonging to the
mendicant orders were in the Duke's train. Unfortunately the trial came to nothing, for before Wycliffe
could open his mouth, the court was broken up by
a rude brawl between his protectors and William
Courtenay, the bishop of London. The citizens would

not endure to see their Bishop insulted in his own
church, and a riot ensued.   John of Gaunt's palace in
the Savoy would, we are told, have been destroyed but
for the generous intervention of the Bishop.   Wycliffe,
personally innocent, may well have suffered in credit
by the behaviour of his friends, but of this nothing is
recorded.   The next proceedings against him were the
issue of negotiations which must have been set on foot
some time before the affair at St. Paul's.   The result
appeared in the promulgation of five Papal bulls against
his teaching.   The first rumour of them reached Wycliffe, as he himself tells us (*De Ecclesia,* ch. xv.), from
the mouth of the Bishop of Rochester in Parliament.
Wycliffe apparently was there in his quality of royal
chaplain, and the date must be earlier than March 2,
when the session ended.[1]   But the bulls themselves
were not actually issued for near three months.

In January 1377 Gregory the Eleventh had entered Rome and terminated the exile of Avignon;
towards the end of May he issued the bulls
against Wycliffe: so that the restoration of
the Roman Papacy is almost coincident with
the beginning of the campaign against the chief assailant of those abuses in the Church system which had
grown to their maturity during the exile.   Three of the
bulls were addressed to the Archbishop of Canterbury
and the Bishop of London, one to the University of
Oxford, and one to the King.   Enclosed was a list of
eighteen 'conclusions' taken from Wycliffe's writings—
in some copies they are enlarged to nineteen ;—if
found guilty of maintaining them he was to be im-

*Papal Bulls
against
Wycliffe.*

---

[1] The next Parliament met on October 13.

prisoned and to await the Pope's sentence. The bulls expressly affirmed Wycliffe's intellectual lineage ; he was following in the error of Marsiglio of Padua : and the articles with which he was charged relate solely to the questions agitated between Church and State, how far the Church's censures could lawfully affect a man's civil position, and whether the Church could rightly receive and hold temporal endowments. The main points in these conclusions are as follow :

I.–V. No man can grant anything to another and to his descendants in perpetuity : possession and the right to possess depend upon a man's being in a state of grace.

VI. If the Church fail in its duty, the temporal lords may rightly and lawfully deprive it of its temporal possessions ; the judgement of such failure lying not with the theologian but with the civil politician.

VII.–X. The mere act of the Pope, or of the Pope and cardinals, has of itself no power either to enable or to disable any man. Excommunication is of no effect unless its object be already self-excommunicated [by his sin]; it ought never to be exercised except upon offenders against the law of Christ.

XI., XII. There is no warrant in the practice of Christ and his disciples for excommunicating a man for the withholding of temporal goods, nor have his disciples now-a-days the power to enforce temporal exactions by ecclesiastical censures.

XIII., XIV. The Pope, or whosoever pretends to ' bind ' and ' loose,' only ' binds ' and ' looses ' so far as he conforms himself to the law of Christ.

XV. Every duly ordained priest has the power of

conferring the sacraments, and thus also of absolving the penitent.

XVI., XVII. repeat in stronger language assertions already contained in earlier articles : the King has a right to deprive churchmen of their property if they habitually misuse it ; all grants being conditional, no matter who made them, it is lawful to take them away if they are improperly used.

XVIII. A churchman, yea, the Roman Pontiff himself, may be rightly rebuked and even arraigned by his subjects and by laymen.

The death of King Edward the Third on the 21st June necessarily prevented any immediate action being taken against Wycliffe ; nor indeed was the time favourable. Though John of Gaunt was not in the new council of government, the Princess of Wales, who had the natural charge of the young King, seems to have been not less favourably disposed towards Wycliffe. As soon as Parliament met he was consulted by it as to the right of withholding the national treasure from passing out of the country even at the Pope's demand ; a right which he supported in a state-paper still extant, which does not read as the work of a man who anticipated serious proceedings against him.[1] He admits the possibility that the Pope might lay England under an interdict in the event of its refusal, just as he had laid Florence a year earlier ; but such a proceeding would be of no effect : ' Supposing that the disciple of Antichrist should break forth into such madness, it is one comfort that censures of this sort

Wycliffe's credit with Parliament.

---

[1] It is printed in the *Fasciculi Zizaniorum*, 258-271.

are not binding in the eyes of God.' It would be a misreading of this passage to infer that Wycliffe had already learned to associate the name of Antichrist with the Pope. Should he take such action, Wycliffe says, he would be the disciple of Antichrist, but he has just before stated his conviction that ' our most holy father' would not do anything so unreasonable. Nevertheless it is plain that Wycliffe was, not unnaturally, moved by the condemnation of his opinions, and at the same time that he relied with assurance on the support of Parliament. Was it likely that it should consult him on a matter so intimately affecting the rights of the Papacy, and yet allow him to suffer for the expression of his general opinions on the subject? Accordingly with full confidence he laid his answer to the Pope's bull before the House.[1] Nor had he misreckoned the drift of English opinion; for, although no immediate steps are known to have been taken by Parliament on his behalf, we find it next year again invoking his advice, and when the critical moment of his trial arrived it was the Princess of Wales—the virtual regent—herself who ordered the proceedings to be stopped.

The Pope had indeed unwittingly succeeded in harassing a variety of ' interests.' The Court had no Proceedings wish to lose a useful and devoted servant; against him. the people of England to a great extent felt that Wycliffe, even though in some ways he might be in error, was really fighting their battle; and the University of Oxford was angry that a distinguished member of its body should be attacked, and chafed still

---

[1] Printed in the *Fasciculi Zizaniorum*, 245-257.

more at the invasion of its privileges threatened by the
subsequent action of the bishops.   For the Archbishop
of Canterbury and the Bishop of London, instead of
simply demanding Wycliffe's arrest, ordered that an
December 18,   enquiry   should   be   held   by   the   Oxford
1377.   divines, and that Wycliffe should be sent
on to be heard in person in London.   The Oxford
masters on the other hand, who had at first hesitated
to receive the bull at all, some maintaining that the
Pope had no right to order any man's imprisonment
in England, finally resolved merely to enjoin Wycliffe
to keep within the walls of Black Hall until they had
come to a decision with respect to his opinions.   The
judgement was that the articles recited in the Papal
bull were orthodox (*veras*), but so expressed as to be
susceptible of an incorrect meaning, a judgement doubtless determined quite as much by academical feeling
as by theological considerations.   Still this did not free
Wycliffe from the obligation of appearing in London,
and the result might have been unfavourable had not
the Princess of Wales sent a messenger on the eve of
the appointed day, early in 1378, to forbid the bishops
to give sentence against him.   Wycliffe appeared in the
chapel of Lambeth Palace, but while the bishops were
anxiously pondering how to obey the Pope without
offending the Princess of Wales, the session was cut
short by an inroad of the London citizens with a crowd
of the rabble at their heels, and Wycliffe escaped either
scotfree or at most with a mild *request* that he would
speak no more touching the conclusions in question.[1]

[1] So substantially the continuation of the *Eulogium Historiarum*, 3,
347 f., and the St. Alban's chronicle given in the *Chronicon Angliæ*,

It was a singular turn in popular feeling which changed Wycliffe from a hireling of the Duke of Lancaster into a sort of national champion; and we can hardly be wrong in thinking that his report to Parliament concerning Papal demands for money had a good deal to do with the change.

However this may be, Wycliffe returned to his old work and abated nothing of his vigour in the defence of what he considered the pure doctrine of the Church, a defence which necessarily involved an attack upon other doctrines and practices which he believed to be false and injurious. Immediately after the affair at Lambeth, occurred the schism in the Papacy which did more than anything to hasten his movement towards the position of a more radical reformer. It will be convenient therefore here to interrupt the story of his life in order to consider the nature of the opinions which he had formed previously to that determining crisis, not in his career only, but in the history of mediæval Christendom.

173 f., 183, and in Walsingham's *Historia Anglicana*, I, 345, 356. Those who speak of Wycliffe as having been enjoined to silence at St. Paul's a year earlier rely on chronicles which confuse the two hearings (*e.g.* the continuation of the *Polychronicon* printed at the end of Mr. Maunde Thompson's edition of the *Chronicon Angliæ*, 396 f.).

CHAPTER VI.

WYCLIFFE'S EARLIER DOCTRINE.

WYCLIFFE'S writings are principally lectures, sermons, and short tracts written for special occasions. With Wycliffe's the exception of two works written in the writings. form of dialogue, there is not one of his productions of any considerable length that can be shown to have been originally written in the shape in which we have it, that is to say, as an independent literary composition. So far as they have been published, all the books that make up his *Summa*—many of which form substantial volumes when printed—were written as lectures, some perhaps in part as sermons; and sometimes they include shorter tracts which originally stood by themselves. Wycliffe wrote as the occasion required, and put together what materials he had ready to hand quite without regard to literary exigencies. Hence it is natural that his writings should be full of repetitions, should cover the same ground more than once, and should be generally defective in arrangement. But this is only true when we look at them as complete books: their separate parts are severely drawn up according to logical rules, coördinated and subdivided in manifold-wise according to the taste of the schools; only unfortunately this same taste demanded that the same points should be proved and re-proved, distinctions invented, analogies forced, and the real scope of the book industriously, as it were, concealed from view.

These characteristics are indeed what we expect in the age of the extreme debasement of the scholastic method, when logic had ceased to act as a stimulus to the intellectual powers and had become rather a clog upon their exercise, and when men no longer framed syllogisms to develop their thoughts, but argued first and thought, if at all, afterwards. The course of the main argument is perpetually interrupted; there are digressions, meanderings, excursions, innumerable: we seem to be moving rapidly, but we soon discover that we are moving in a circle. Such are the limitations of the world of thought in which Wycliffe lived. His formal treatment is of the poorest and most wearisome description: it is only when we reach the special points which he set himself to prove, and which he thought he proved by means of all these clumsy processes, that we at all realise the intellectual vigour which, in spite of his method, Wycliffe possessed in no contemptible degree, although it is no doubt vain to compare him with the greatest thinkers of the Middle Ages. To the faults of his method too must be added those of his style. His Latinity is that of a time when scholars were ceasing to *think* in Latin. It is significant of his position that he is one of the founders of English prose-writing; indeed often the readiest way of understanding an obscure passage is to translate it into English. We admire, while we can hardly understand, the devotion which moved his disciples laboriously to transcribe his crabbed treatises in such numbers that, after all that burning and confiscation has done, they still exist, mostly in several copies, in the libraries of Vienna, Prague, and other places on the Continent, as well as in the English Universities, at Dublin, Lambeth, and elsewhere. We refer solely to Wycliffe's Latin works; and of these it is not necessary to go beyond his works *On the Lordship of God* and *On Civil Lordship*, in order to obtain a clear view of the essential part of his teaching prior to the schism of 1378. His earliest productions, philosophical treatises of a purely scholastic character, need not be more than mentioned. Only one has as yet found its way into print, and this is believed by its editor to represent the mere notes of his lectures taken by one of his scholars.[1]

When he passed to theology he did not, so far as is known, for many years run counter to the received His theological opinions of the Church. The impulse which work. led him further may be clearly traced to the teaching of Richard FitzRalph, Archbishop of Armagh, who had been a Fellow of Balliol College some years before Wycliffe himself. FitzRalph's attack upon the mendicant orders had proceeded from a denial of their special doctrine of 'evangelical poverty' to the development of a general theory of the relation of God to man which he formulated in the term *dominium* or 'lordship'. Wycliffe borrowed the conception from him, but endeavoured to combine it with the very doctrine of poverty against which his master had written.

[1] *De compositione hominis*, edited by R. Beer, 1884.

Nothing is stranger than the way in which Ockham
adopts the doctrine of poverty to assail the hierarchy,
FitzRalph denies it to assail the friars, and Wycliffe
combines the essence of both arguments to carry on the
attack of Ockham;—unless it be the way in which ultimately Wycliffe came over to a practical application of
FitzRalph's position, which he could use without reserve
against friars and monks, and the whole external fabric of
the Roman Church. This stage we have not yet reached.
At present Wycliffe is on excellent terms with the friars;
it was members of their orders who supported him in
his abortive trial at St. Paul's, and he never misses an
opportunity of saying a good word for them. His attack
is directed against Church endowments, and specially
against the ' possessioners,' the monks who add house
to house and field to field, and to the friars only who follow in their ill example. It is the wealth of the Church
that he cannot away with, the seeking after temporal
goods and temporal dignities, the interference of the
Church with secular aims and occupations. And to
reason out his position he worked upon the foundation
of FitzRalph and produced his doctrine of ' lordship.'

Lordship and service, in Wycliffe's scheme, are the
two ends of the chain that links humanity to God;
Doctrine of lordship. they are necessarily correspondent terms,
and the one cannot exist without the other.
A man may have a right, or may have power, although
he can exercise neither; he cannot have lordship, which
includes the notion both of right and power, unless
there is something over which he is lord. God himself was not God until after the creation, a fact which
is shown, Wycliffe considers, by the employment of

the distinctive name first in the second chapter of
Genesis. But God's lordship is of a unique character
because, all being his creatures, all owe him service,
and all alike. Here we reach the essential inference
which brings Wycliffe's theory into connexion with
practical life. 'God rules not mediately through the
rule of subject vassals, as other kings hold lordship,
since immediately and of himself he makes, sustains,
and governs all that which he possesses, and helps it
to perform its works according to other uses which he
requires.'[1] There is a feudalism here, but a feudalism
in which there are no mesne lords; all men 'hold'
directly of God, with differences no doubt in accidentals,
but in the main fact of their tenure all alike. ⟩

It is this principle of the dependence of the individual man upon God alone and upon none else that distin-
guishes Wycliffe's from any other system of the Middle
Ages. He alone ventured to strike at the root of the
hierarchical privilege by vindicating for each separate
person an equal place in the eyes of God. By this
formula all laymen became priests, and all priests laymen, so far as their religious position was concerned:
all held of God, and on the same terms of service.
Yet it is clear that the principle by itself was one
acknowledged by every Christian; it was Wycliffe's
application of it that made it peculiar and dangerous.
What he did was to transfer the conception from the
religious to the political sphere. The rank which a
man has in the eyes of God must involve his rank,
consequence, position, all that he is or has, in the eyes
of men. If by sin he forfeits the former, necessarily

---

[1] *De dominio divino,* i. 5 (MS.).

also the latter goes with it. The result was that Wycliffe was led into a variety of paradoxes akin to those of the early Anabaptists or of the Shakers of our own day. These are shown clearly in his book *On Civil Lordship.*

He begins the book with the proposition that no one in mortal sin has any right to any gift of God, while on the other hand every man standing in grace has not only a right to, but has in fact, every gift of God. He takes literally the aphorism which an old tradition inserted in the Book of Proverbs, *The faithful man hath the whole world of riches, but the unfaithful hath not even a farthing ;*[1] and he supports it with much fulness and ingenuity of argumentation. The first part of the thesis is indeed a legitimate following out of the doctrine which Saint Augustin had enforced, of the negative character of evil. *Sin,* he said, *is nothing, and men, when they sin, become nothing :* if then, argued Wycliffe, sinners, as such, are nothing, it is evident that they can possess nothing. Moreover, possession presupposes a right or title to possess ; and this right or title can only be held ultimately to depend upon the good pleasure of God, who plainly cannot be thought to approve the lordship of the wicked or the manner in which they abuse their power. Again, by the common law an inferior lord may not alienate real property without the license of his lord-in-chief and any grant in contravention of his will is wrongful ; accordingly, as God is the lord-in-chief of

[1] Placed in the Septuagint after Prov. xvii. 6 or 4 (in different manuscripts), and quoted by SS. Jerom and Augustin. See Wycliffe, *De civili dominio,* i. 7, 12, &c.

all human beings, it should appear that any grant made to a sinner must be contrary to his will, and thus be no real or proper possession at all. But even granting that the sinner can have such possession, all lordship is conferred by God on the consideration of a man's returning to him continually due service: when however a man falls into mortal sin he defrauds his lord-in-chief of this service, and thus rightfully incurs forfeiture and is deprived of all lordship whatsoever.

How then does the wicked man come to have property in earthly things? Wycliffe's explanation turns on the double meaning of the word *Church*, considered either as the holy spouse of Christ or as, in its transitory condition, the human society mixed of good and evil. To the Church in its ideal signification God makes the grant; the wicked have their share only by virtue of their outward membership of it. But since the sole sufficient title to possession is the immediate grant of God, it results that such possession as the wicked have is not worthy to be called possession at all: and *Whosoever hath not, from him shall be taken even that which he seemeth to have.*

By means of this and similar texts of Scripture the way is prepared for Wycliffe's second main proposition, namely, that the righteous is lord of all things, or in precise terms 'the righteous man is lord over the whole sensible world.' If a man has anything, he has everything, for God cannot give anything except he give abundantly. Thus, even when the righteous is afflicted in this life, he still has true possession of the whole universe, inasmuch as *all*

Community of goods.

things work together for good to him, in assisting him
towards eternal happiness. It would be impossible to
indicate the spiritual nature of the lordship claimed by
Wycliffe for the righteous, more distinctly than by this
example : yet he proceeds to dwell upon its literal
truth in a way that might almost persuade us that he
is really developing a system of polity applicable to
the existing conditions of life. He pursues his doctrine to the logical conclusion that, as there are many
righteous, and each is lord of the universe, all goods
must necessarily be held in common. He has no
doubt or hesitation about this doctrine of community :
he avows it plainly as a Christian application of the
' Socratic,' that is the Platonic, doctrine, excluding
only the Greek corollary that wives should be held in
common. At the same time it may be inferred from
several guarding sentences that his aim was not to
favour a communistic reorganisation of the State, at
least in the present conditions of society, but rather
to look forward to such a change as a future ideal.

Passing back to the elements of Wycliffe's theory of
lordship, we have seen that it has two sides to it : on
the one, the righteous has all things ; on the other,
the wicked has nothing, and only occupies for a time
that which he has unrighteously usurped or stolen
from the righteous. In Wycliffe's favourite phrase,
lordship is 'founded in grace ;' and grace (or, from
another point of view, the law of the Gospel) being
alone essential to it, it follows necessarily that human
ordinances are accidental or indifferent. The whole
system of civil society appears to Wycliffe the mere
consequence of the fall of man : it originated in sin,

in 'the lust of lordship,' and for the most part it betrays its origin evidently enough by the opportunities it affords for wrongdoing and tyranny. Wycliffe singularly enough adopts the point of view which had been emphasised for a very different object by Pope Gregory the Seventh nearly three hundred years before. He has not, as Saint Thomas Aquinas had, the philosopher's insight which could recognise a human law as something inextricably involved in the existence of a human society. With Wycliffe therefore, while natural lordship is that of the Gospel and so eternal, civil lordship is but transitory and liable to modification according to the changes of human society. It becomes therefore to Wycliffe a matter of slight importance, what particular form of government be adopted in any given country, since its only claim to excellence depends upon its relation with 'natural lordship,' in other words with the precepts of religion. Like Ockham, Wycliffe feels too strongly the necessary infirmity of all human institutions to be able to lay down any fixed scheme of government. He suspects all principles almost in the same degree, the popular will, hereditary or elective monarchy; and seems to give a grudging preference to monarchy of the hereditary class chiefly because it was the system under which he lived and which he found on the whole to work well. 'It appears to me,' he says,[1] 'that the discreet theologian will determine nothing rashly as touching these laws, but according to law will affirm that it were better that all things should be had in common.'

But lordship, as was stated at the outset, has

[1] *De civili dominio,* i. 30.

another aspect to it; the theory of the community
of lordship in itself involves its counterpart, the community of service. In this we find the only check
recognised by Wycliffe upon the action of kings : they
have a responsibility, not so much to the people over
whom they rule as to God from whom they derive
their lordship. They are his stewards, and lords only
by virtue of service. God is the only lord whose
dominion is unattended by this condition ; all others
are servants not only of God but also of all their fellow-men. The Pope himself is named in his own
letters 'the servant of the servants of God.' It is
the corollary of this, that all things, all that we call
property, must belong in common to all. Wycliffe
had not yet learned the effect of his doctrine in practical life, as displayed in the rebellion of 1381 ; but
he seems conscious of the danger of excusing by implication desultory attempts of this nature, when he warns
his hearers against resort to force except it be likely to
put an end to tyranny.

Yet, examining his words carefully, we cannot but
admit that his conception is really not only spiritual
in its sphere but also prospective, not present, in its
application. The opposition between the righteous
who have all things and the unrighteous who have
nothing remains throughout the text of Wycliffe's dis-
course. In it he finds the secret of the differences of
human lot; by its means he is able to reconcile the
prosperity of the wicked with the troubles and disap-
pointments of the good. He translates the Bible into
the language of feudalism, and then having satisfied
himself that Christianity and lordship are convertible

terms, he proceeds to explain his new-found polity on
a strictly spiritual basis. But however ideal the principle on which Wycliffe goes, it has none the less a
very plain meaning when applied to the circumstances
of the religious organism in the writer's own time.
For the essence of the whole conception lies in the
stress which he laid upon inner, as opposed to outer,
elements as those which determine a man's proper
merit. To Wycliffe, it was the personal relation, the
immediate dependence of the individual man upon God,
that made him worthy or unworthy; it was his own
character, and not his office, that constituted him what
he really was. The Pope himself, if a bad man, lost
his entire right to lordship.

Wycliffe may seem to contradict himself when he
says at one moment that sin deprives a man of all
right to rule, and at another that we ought
to yield a passive obedience even to tyrants.
He felt no doubt that, as things are, the
spheres of spiritual and temporal sovereignty are kept
asunder; and thus was driven to conclude that each
held good, so far as the present state of affairs was
concerned, although in the eternal order of the universe right, power, lordship, and the practical exercise
of authority, could only depend on the righteousness of
the person to whom they belonged. Hence Wycliffe
was led to the same position with regard to the Church
as Marsiglio and Ockham. With them he felt that
the Church suffered in its spiritual worth by being
brought into connexion with secular affairs and interests. 'For to rule temporal possessions after a
civil manner, to conquer kingdoms and exact tributes,

Severance of spiritual and temporal.

appertain to earthly lordship, not to the Pope; so that
if he pass by and set aside the office of spiritual rule,
and entangle himself in those other concerns, his work
is not only superfluous but also contrary to holy Scripture.'[1] Yet Wycliffe was at present as far as any man
from desiring to impair the dignity or influence of the
Pope. It is because he was persuaded that this was
incompatible with the business of the external world,
that he urged its separation from such entanglement.

When however the two powers crossed one another
Wycliffe could not but hold that right was on the side
of the temporal interest. When the Church exercised
functions which justly belonged to the State, when it
became involved in transactions about money and territorial possession, then, he maintained, it was time for
the State to interfere and vindicate its rights over its
own affairs. The misused revenues of the Church were
to be reclaimed and the spiritualty was to be limited
to its proper spiritual office. Wycliffe earnestly be-
seeches his hearers not to understand him as though
he meant that such a case had actually arisen; but
the very argument by which he excuses himself from
deciding this was one that only added to the perilous-
ness of his doctrine in the eyes of official theologians,
since it was not with them, he declared, that the decision of the issue lay, but with politicians who had
practical experience of government. He goes through
the whole set of burning questions thus raised; and
his answers, however guarded in their expression, and
however much he may protect himself by ingenious
quotations from the canon law, are unmistakeable in

[1] *De civili dominio,* i. 17.

their import. Is it right to excommunicate a man if he refuses, for instance, to pay tithes ? Excommunication is only the formal statement of the condition of a man who by his own act, that is, by sin, has placed himself *extra communionem ecclesiæ ;* if he has not sinned, the excommunication is null and void. Saint Gregory himself enjoined that no clergyman should excommunicate a man for a personal injury done to himself. In the case of tithes a man is bound not to pay them to a wicked parson, who through his evil-doing has lost all claim to his share of them ; the rest is due to the poor, and this the layman may as well in such a case pay to the poor directly.

If however excommunication is simply one's own doing, merely pronounced *ex post facto* by the Church, what becomes of the power of the keys ?—
The power of the keys. *Whatsoever thou shalt bind on earth shall be bound in heaven,* &c. Evidently, is Wycliffe's reply, no power can be granted to man except subject to the will of God. If any act of the Pope's is wrong, it is invalid. Here Wycliffe repeats the famous answer of Robert Grosseteste, Bishop of Lincoln, to Innocent the Fourth, when he made what the Bishop considered to be an immoral use of his patronage : ' Apostolic commands I obey, but those which
1253. oppose the commands of the apostles I withstand.' Robert Grosseteste refused to believe that such an act, such an ' abominable sin,' as that which professed to be that of Pope Innocent really proceeded from the apostolic See ; and consequently he openly resisted the mandate. His loyalty to the Church was undoubted, and he lost nothing by this refusal ; the letter to the Pope

was the best known and the most widely circulated of his writings, and it furnished a precedent to later opponents of the Papal power. Nor, be it observed, does Wycliffe go beyond it: he maintains just what Bishop Robert had maintained, that the decree of the Pope is binding so far, and so far only, as it is agreeable to the will of God as expressed in his word. He has no scruple in obeying the present Pope, of whom he speaks in language of devotion ; but supposing he should ordain anything contrary to holy Scripture, Wycliffe declares that he and all true Christians are bound to disobey him.

That the Pope may fall into sin is as essential a part of Wycliffe's doctrine as it was of Ockham's. More than this, he has already arrived at the conclusion that the Pope is no necessary element in the constitution of the Christian Church, however desirable his existence may be. With that deep-rooted distrust of human arrangements, which again he seems to have derived from Ockham, Wycliffe not only maintains that Pope and cardinals might conceivably be dispensed with, but even says that he can imagine a state of society in which the Church should consist solely of laymen. He is evidently far on the road which led him to his later, what may be called his protestant, position. Anxious as he is to defend himself by the maxims of canon law, and anxious not to go beyond the Church tradition as he finds it in the earlier and greater of the fathers, he is constrained to oppose to its later developments his fundamental principle that the ' law of the gospel,' the doctrine of holy Scripture, is the sole and absolute rule of the Christian

C. H. G

Church.   Possibly Wycliffe was unhistorical, possibly
he was going backwards instead of forwards ; and yet
when we consider the way in which the growth of the
Papacy had seemed in recent times to be acting, not
only in hostility to the national growth of the countries of Europe, but also to their moral advancement,
we cannot but confess that the reformer had some
reason on his side.   He may not have seen the right
direction towards which the Church should be guided,
but he did what he could ; he set up one plain rule of
life in opposition to that which in his time held its
ground : against the sacerdotal or hierarchical system,
he put forward the evangelical.   And up to this stage
the national instinct of religious Englishmen went
largely with him.

CHAPTER VII.

WYCLIFFE AND THE GREAT SCHISM.

WYCLIFFE'S first appearance in public affairs after the proceedings connected with the Papal bulls of con-
Question of Sanctuary.
demnation was in the autumn parliament of 1378. John of Gaunt had violated the sanctuary of Westminster by sending a band of armed men to seize two knights who had taken refuge there. It is not necessary here to go further into the circumstances than to say that they were complicated by some considerations of foreign policy brought about by the duke's pretension to the throne of Castile. The knights offered resistance, and in the fray that ensued one of them was killed. After an interval of dismay the Bishop of London summoned courage to excommunicate all concerned in the outrage (excepting only by name the King, his mother, and the Duke of Lancaster) and preached vigorously against the culprits at Saint Paul's Cross. The duke fearing the anger of the Londoners arranged that the next Parliament should be held at a safe distance, at Gloucester, and, it was rumoured, proposed to revenge himself upon the bishop by bringing before it a sweeping scheme for secularising Church property. Wycliffe was called upon to

write a defence of the duke's action at Westminster.
This paper, which is still preserved · and incorporated
in the treatise *De Ecclesia*,[1] seeks to lay down the
limits within which the privilege of sanctuary is per-
missible, and maintains that the duke was right in
invading the sanctuary in order to bring escaped
prisoners to justice ; it was they who began the attack
and so the duke's officers cannot be blamed for the
bloodshed which ensued.   Wycliffe points out that
the canon law itself admits exceptions to the universal
privilege of sanctuary, and urges fairly enough that
the privilege is one specially liable to be abused to
the injury of society and the public peace.   At the
same time, when it is borne in mind that the violation of the sanctuary was the last stage in a series of
high-handed acts done by John of Gaunt in the matter, one cannot help feeling that it was not a good
case for argument on general grounds, and that
Wycliffe did not raise his reputation by undertaking
its defence.

This year 1378 forms a turning-point in the reformer's life.   On March 27 Pope Gregory the Eleventh
The Papal   died ; his successor Urban the Sixth was
schism.   elected, April 7.   The French members of
the cardinals' college were highly dissatisfied at the
return of the curia to Italy ; and the violent, tyrannical
behaviour of the new Pope soon brought matters to
a crisis.   The validity of his election was called in

[1] The subject is discussed at large from ch. vii. to xvi. inclusive ;
but apparently only ch. vii., which exists in manuscript in a separate
form, is the actual state paper, unless indeed the whole section (ch.
vii.–xvi.) be not an elaboration of this.

57953

question; it was declared void, and in September an Antipope was chosen, who took the style of Clement the Seventh. Attachment to one or the other of the two claimants very soon became a question of nationality. Clement was naturally supported by France, and France followed by the Spanish kingdoms, Naples, and Scotland; while England and the north (Flanders, Germany, Bohemia, Hungary, and Poland), as well as Portugal, remained loyal to Urban. For nearly half a century there were two lines of Popes, Urban and his successors holding their own in Rome, or at least in the greater part of Italy, while Clement returned to Avignon and continued the tradition of the Babylonian exile.

It was the Great Schism which changed Wycliffe from a critic to a declared opponent of the Papacy. Wycliffe's poor But in this change there were stages. First, priests. it seems, he was mainly occupied in making his gospel known among the people of England at large. He set on foot an irregular body of itinerant preachers, and supplied them with an English Bible to direct their teaching. Neither of these schemes appears to have excited any immediate suspicion among churchmen. The 'poor priests' were not necessarily intended to conflict with the rights of the beneficed clergy. The conception that lay at the root of the institution was practically the same as that which had inspired the founders of the great mendicant orders. Nor again were the 'simple priests' or 'poor preachers' whom Wycliffe sent out over England as a rule illiterate men. Some of them no doubt were, but many were Fellows of Oxford colleges and some seem

to have enjoyed high respect in the University. The
main principle on which they were designed to act
was to supplement the services of the Church, which,
held as they were in a language not understood of the
people, tended to become a lifeless formality, by regular
religious instruction in their mother-tongue. In this
aim Wycliffe was really carrying out a well-known
tendency of his age. In 1362 it was ordered that
English should be used in the courts of law. In 1363
the speech of the Chancellor in opening Parliament
was in English; and the practice was thenceforth frequently repeated. In 1381 Archbishop Courtenay, the
Chancellor, opened Parliament with an English sermon,
and Archbishop Thoresby of York was active in pro-
moting the use of the mother-tongue in preaching
and in offices of devotion.[1]

Wycliffe was distinguished from other workers to
the same end by the fact that he not only urged the
The English   use of English but made this use possible
Bible.   by the translation of the Bible which he
planned and superintended, and in great part executed
himself. Parts of the Bible had been done into English long before Wycliffe's time; but Wycliffe was the
first *populariser* as well as the first completer of the
English Bible : and the fact that some hundred and
fifty manuscripts, containing either the whole or some
part of his versions, remain to us in spite of the
vigorous measures taken to suppress them, is evidence
enough of the wide diffusion which those versions
obtained. As for the manner in which the translations were made the following particulars may suffice.

[1] See Stubbs, *Const. Hist. of Engl.,* 2, §§ 259, 264.

Wycliffe himself started with the New Testament: then his disciple Nicholas Hereford began the Old, which appears to have been completed by Wycliffe. Afterwards the whole was revised by John Purvey, his friend and assistant in his parish work at Lutterworth; and this second edition was finished shortly after Wycliffe's death. Naturally it became the accepted text, and nearly all the existing copies are taken from it. In the edition of the work published at Oxford in 1850 under the care of Josiah Forshall and Sir Frederic Madden, Wycliffe's and Purvey's versions are printed in parallel columns. It is hardly necessary to add that the translation was made not from the originals but from the Latin Vulgate.

These labours might seem to have engrossed Wycliffe's energy in the years from 1377 or 1378 onwards; and yet it was during this very time that he produced probably the majority of his numerous writings. It was also during this time that he exposed himself to a definite charge of heresy. The influence of his preachers was quickly felt throughout the country. The common people were rejoiced by the simple and homely doctrine which dwelt chiefly on the plain truths of the Gospel; while the pungent invective which accompanied it added zest to their discontent at the heedless pastors whom they saw too generally about them. The feeling of resentment against the rich clergy, monks, and friars, was widespread but undefined. Wycliffe turned it into a distinct channel,—he was now persuaded that the friars were as bad as the monks;—and his organisation enabled him to scatter his denunciation of them far and wide on a congenial soil. At the same time he insensibly passed from an assailant of the Papal, to an assailant of the sacerdotal,

Wycliffe's denial of transubstantiation. power ; and in this way was led to deny the speaking evidence of that power conveyed in the doctrine of transubstantiation. To Wycliffe as to some of the later reformers the doctrine was objectionable not primarily for theological but for political reasons. Of course he had to support his contention by theological arguments ; but these, it appears to us, were much rather the buttresses than the foundation of his view. He felt deeply that the failings of the Church arose in great measure from the pretensions of the priesthood. They were, he held, abusing their trust when they claimed authority over their brother Christians, since all Christians were equal in the sight of God. To admit therefore that the priest had the power of 'making the body of Christ' (this was the accepted orthodox phrase), was to exalt him to a position irreconcilable with that view of the Church which Wycliffe maintained. Still the doctrine of transubstantiation had been generally accepted in the Western Church for more than five centuries, and had been formally and authoritatively laid down for three. It had been fortified by all the subtle learning of the great schoolmen, and had gradually become the citadel of the priestly power. To take away this power of working a daily miracle was at once and justly felt as the most serious attack upon the whole church-system.

In the summer of 1381 Wycliffe first publicly denied that the elements in the sacrament of the altar suffered any *material* change by virtue of the words of consecration. The real presence of the body and blood of

Christ he entirely believed; what he denied was the change of substance in the host. The heresy was His condemnation at Oxford. promulgated in Oxford, and the Chancellor of the University, William of Berton, was bound to take official cognisance of it. He summoned twelve doctors of theology and law, half the number being friars, to add their weight to a solemn and authoritative decree condemning the new doctrines maintained by 'certain persons filled with the counsel of the evil spirit,' but avoiding the mention of Wycliffe's name. The condemnation was announced to Wycliffe as he was sitting in the schools of Austinfriars in the act of disputing on the subject. He refused to accept the judgement, and made appeal, not, it was remarked, to the Pope or to any bishop—according to the invariable practice in a matter of heretical depravity,—but to the King; whereupon John of Gaunt, whether to protect his old ally or to disclaim any further association with him, promptly sent down a messenger to Oxford, enjoining Wycliffe to say no more on the perilous question. The reformer however continued to maintain his thesis, and was plainly not afraid of the University taking more serious measures against him. It is even possible that the Chancellor's act so strongly excited the feeling of the place that he had soon to resign his office, and was succeeded by one Robert Rygge, who more than inclined to support Wycliffe.[1]

While Wycliffe was thus entering upon his most

[1] The precise order of events is uncertain, since Anthony Wood's dates for the successive chancellors do not allow of Berton's holding the office in 1381, and no materials have yet been discovered for settling the chronology. I suspect that the actual condemnation did not take place until the beginning of 1382.

serious encounter with the established powers of the
Church, perhaps before his teaching was actually condemned by the University, a struggle of a different
kind arose in England, in which it was natural that
The Peasants' men should see the carrying into effect of
Revolt. his revolutionary principles. The peasants
of the Eastern counties rose in arms ; they were joined
by many of the baser sort, and much havock was done.
Archbishop Sudbury was only the most conspicuous of
a large number of victims. There is no evidence to
connect Wycliffe personally with the rising. One of
its leaders, John Ball, indeed made a confession that he
learnt his subversive doctrines from Wycliffe. But the
confession of a condemned man can seldom be accepted
without reserve ; and Ball's assertion is invalidated not
only by the repeated testimony of a contemporary his-
torian, Knyghton, that he was a precursor of Wycliffe,
but also by documentary evidence that he was excommunicated as early as 1366, long before Wycliffe exposed himself to ecclesiastical censure. The fact also, of
which there is no doubt, that the rebels directed their
special hostility against the Duke of Lancaster, is by itself
enough to clear Wycliffe of any complicity in the affair.
Had he not only supported it but also turned against
his old patron, it is hard indeed to understand how it
was that he was not brought up for trial. Wycliffe in
truth was always careful to state his communistic views in
a theoretical way ; they appear moreover to be confined
to his Latin writings. At the same time it is very possible that his less scrupulous followers translated them
in their popular discourses, and thus fed the flame that
burst forth in the revolt of 1381 ; perhaps it was a

consciousness of responsibility in it that led them to cast the blame on the friars. Yet all readers of English history know that there were deeper causes for disaffection in the social state of the country, of themselves sufficient to account for the rebellion, without there being any need to call in the influence of Wycliffe; though on the other hand one might wish that he had more publicly declared his condemnation of the excesses of which he was well aware, a condemnation which is only incidentally expressed in a single passage of his treatise *On Blasphemy*.

When order was again restored, Courtenay who now succeeded Sudbury as Archbishop of Canterbury took *The Earthquake* active measures for repressing Wycliffite *Council.* opinions. He summoned a synod to examine them, and ten bishops and fifty other persons assembled at the Blackfriars in London on the 17th May, 1382. The first session was interrupted by an earthquake, which was differently interpreted as a sign of the divine approval or anger. The Earthquake Council had no choice but to condemn the doctrines; but Wycliffe does not appear to have been present nor any action at all to have been taken against him personally. His good fortune is inexplicable unless we accept the usual explanation that his popularity at Oxford rendered him a formidable person to attack. He was left at peace and the storm fell upon his disciples.

The sequel forms a curious episode in university history. The Archbishop sent down a commissary, *The Oxford* Peter Stokes, to Oxford, with a mandate to *Wycliffites.* prohibit the teaching of incorrect doctrines, but avoiding any mention of the teacher's name. The

University authorities were by no means pleased at this invasion—so they held it—of their ancient privileges. The Chancellor, Rygge, had just appointed Nicholas Hereford, a devoted follower of Wycliffe, to preach before the University: he now appointed a no less loyal follower, Philip Repyngdon, for the same office. Stokes reported that he dared not publish the Archbishop's mandate, that he went about in fear of his life; it appeared that not the Chancellor only but both the proctors were Wycliffites, or at least preferred to support the Wycliffites to abating one jot of what they considered the privileges of the University.   Still, when the Chancellor was summoned before the Archbishop in London he did not venture to disobey; and promptly cleared himself of any suspicion of heresy. The council met again (June 12) at the Blackfriars, and Rygge submissively took his seat in it.   Short work was made of the Oxford Wycliffites: they were generally, and four of them by name (Hereford, Repyngdon, John Aston, and Lawrence Bedeman), suspended from all academical functions.   Rygge returned to Oxford, with a letter from Courtenay which repeated the condemnation of the four preachers, adding to theirs the name of Wycliffe himself.   But the Chancellor protested he dared not execute this mandate, and a royal warrant had to be issued to compel him. Meanwhile he showed his real feeling in the matter by suspending a prominent opponent of the Wycliffites who had called them by the offensive name of 'Lollards.'   But the council in London went on to overpower the party by stronger measures.   Of the four men named, Hereford and Repyngdon, who had sought in vain the protection of John of Gaunt, were excommunicated; Aston and Bedeman condemned as heretics. For a while they hid in the country; but before long they all recanted and were restored to their privileges in the University, with the exception of Hereford who fled to the continent and is believed to have been imprisoned by Pope Urban the Sixth. The Wycliffite party at Oxford was not however extinguished. Academical feeling probably went quite as far as personal attachment to Wycliffe in keeping it alive and vigorous; and the most stringent measures of Archbishop Arundel a quarter of a century later were necessary to break its strength once for all. But so repressive was the policy of Arundel that the overthrow of Wycliffism involved also that of the intellectual independence of the University itself. The history of Oxford for more than a century to come is a history of almost unrelieved decline in learning, morals, and religion.

Wycliffe's opinions were thus condemned, but no attempt seems to have been made to bring Wycliffe Wycliffe's last years. himself to judgement. He remained at large and unmolested. It is said indeed that he appeared before a council held by Archbishop Courtenay at Oxford, and made a recantation; but our single authority for the statement fortunately gives the text of the recantation, which proves to be nothing more nor less than a plain English statement of the condemned doctrine. It is therefore lawful to doubt whether Wycliffe appeared before the council at all, and even whether he was summoned before it. Probably after the overthrow of his party at Oxford by the Blackfriars Council Wycliffe found it advisable to withdraw permanently to

Lutterworth.   That his strength among the laity was
undiminished is shown by the fact that an ordinance
suppressing his itinerant preachers passed by the Lords
alone in May 1382 was annulled on the petition of
the Commons in the following autumn ; while it is at
least curious to note that on the meeting of the previous Parliament in May, on the very eve of the Blackfriars' Council, he was not afraid to address a memorial
to the Parliament in favour of a drastic measure of
church-reform.   In London, Leicester, and elsewhere,
there is abundant evidence of his popularity.   The
reformer however was growing old ; there was work
for him to do more lasting than personal controversy ;
and thus in his retirement he occupied himself with
restless activity in writing numerous tracts, English
and Latin, as well as one of his most important books,
the *Trialogus.*   In 1383 a crusade was ordered
by Pope Urban against his rival, and Bishop Henry
Despenser of Norwich led an expedition into Flanders
which ended after a few months in a somewhat inglorious collapse.   Wycliffe, to whom both Popes were
equally obnoxious, made use of the opportunity to
write one of his most effective tracts, *The Crusade,*
in which he denounced the perversion of a sacred mission to the purposes of a war started by means of prodigal offers of indulgence and sustained by the greed
for plunder and the inveterate hatred of Englishmen
for France.   In this line of argument at least he was
likely to win, as he deserved, the approval of wise and
moderate men, however much they might resent his
attitude towards the Papacy.   At last Pope Urban
cited him to answer for his opinions before him at

Rome: but the summons came too late. Wycliffe had already in 1382 or 1383 suffered a paralytic seizure which lamed him; he worked on until on the 28th December 1384, while he was hearing mass, he received a final stroke from which he died on New Year's eve. He was buried at Lutterworth; but by a decree of the Council of Constance, May 4, 1415, his remains were ordered to be taken up and cast out, an order which was executed more than twelve years later by Bishop Fleming, the founder of Lincoln College, Oxford.

Note on Wycliffe's Writings.

Wycliffe's earlier works without exception, together with a large number of his later productions, are written in Latin; and comparatively few of these are preserved in England. They were mostly carried by devoted students into Bohemia, some of whom were at the pains of transcribing entire works from borrowed copies in England before their return home. Such store was set by them that there are still existing three careful catalogues of the entire Latin works made early in the fifteenth century. In Bohemia the books suffered in the common proscription of dangerous literature; they were seized by the ecclesiastical power and placed for safe custody in monasteries; whence, by the irony of fate, they passed, through the secularising measures of the last century, into the public libraries of Prague, Vienna, and other places. Until lately the only works published were the *Trialogus,* printed (apparently at Basle) in 1525, and again at Frankfurt in 1753, and rëedited from the manuscripts by Professor Gotthard Victor Lechler at Oxford in 1869; the tract *De Officio Pastorali* edited by the same scholar at Leipzig in 1863; and a few minor pieces. In 1882 the Wyclif Society was founded in London, chiefly through the energy of Mr. F. J. Furnivall and Mr. F. D. Matthew, for the purpose of publishing a complete edition of those works which still lay in manuscript. Its publications up to the present time are two volumes of *Polemical*

Tracts, edited by Dr. Rudolf Buddensieg (also issued at Leipzig); *De Dominio Civili liber I.,* edited by the writer of the present volume ; *De Ecclesia,* edited by Professor J. Loserth, who has also published two volumes, and nearly completed a third, of the *Sermons ;* the *Dialogus,* edited by Mr. A. W. Pollard , *De Incarnatione Verbi,* edited by Dr. E. Harris; and *De Compositione Hominis,* edited by Dr. Rudolf Beer.

The English works were, partly no doubt on account of their greater literary interest, published earlier. Besides the *Wicket* (a sermon on the Sacrament) which was published in 1546 and has been more than once reprinted, several tracts were edited by Dr. James early in the seventeenth, and Dr. Todd and Dr. Robert Vaughan in the present century. Practically all that Wycliffe wrote in English (except the *Wicket*), together with a good deal that is doubtful or spurious, has been collected in the *Select English Works* edited by Mr. Thomas Arnold, in three volumes, Oxford 1869-1871, and the *English Works hitherto unpublished,* edited by Mr. F. D. Matthew for the Early English Text Society in 1880.

CHAPTER VIII.

LOLLARDY IN ENGLAND AND BOHEMIA.

THE narrative of Wycliffe's life brings clearly before
us the two main principles for which he strove : first,

Meaning of
Lollardy. the political aim to free the Church from
its connexion with temporal affairs and in-
terests ; and secondly, the scheme of doctrinal reform
resting upon the substitution of the 'law of the gospel' for the tradition of the Church. The former
principle, so far as it was bound up with his view of
the desirability of a communistic state of society, died
out, in its practical bearings, with the peasants' revolt
of 1381 ; but its further issues, ripening into a
complete attack upon the existing constitution of the
Church, became so closely allied with the attack upon
established doctrines that it is impossible any longer
to keep them separate. A Wycliffite or Lollard comes
to indicate one who opposes the hierarchical organisation and the temporal endowments of the Church,
together with a number of specific doctrines among
which that of transubstantiation is the most prominent ; who maintains the duty of public preaching as paramount among the obligations of the
Christian minister, and the duty of reading the Bible

as necessary alike for the layman and the clergy-man.

For a number of years these views obtained a wide currency in England. It is impossible to deny that Repressive measures. the failings of the established churchmen, not to speak of the general scandal caused by the schism in the Papacy, gave considerable excuse, if not justification, for their prevalence. But to allow them free circulation was a course open to serious question in the then existing state of religious opinion. The doctrine of the Catholic Church on the subject was the same as that of the Reformed Church under Henry the Eighth, the same as that of the Puritan colonies in New England in the seventeenth century : *it* was the only true Church, and whoever dissented did so at his peril. It may even be doubted whether persecution, as we now hold it, was not the only consistent and the only conscientious course that could be pursued with regard to the Lollards ; the offending member must be sacrificed for the good of the whole body politic. Still humane instincts had raised a scruple as to the means applicable for the purpose, and one cannot but regret that the penalty of death for heresy should have been introduced into England at a time when the Church did not present that spectacle of union and wholesome use of its resources which might seem to justify its exclusion of alternative methods. The penalty had indeed been authorised for near two centuries on the continent of Europe, and it had not yet been discredited by such abuses as characterised it in a later age. England had not adopted it, because it had not needed it : now that heresy had infected the

land, there seemed no excuse for omitting to use that
remedy which had been deemed suitable by Christendom at large; and, (as we shall see immediately,) in
1389 the penalty of death was officially used as a
threat—it proved a sufficient threat—several years
before it was legalised by statute.

The extent to which Wycliffism prevailed in England in the time immediately succeeding the reformer's
death cannot be ascertained. To say with
Knyghton that every other man you met in
the streets was a Wycliffite is doubtless an
exaggeration; but it cannot be questioned that the
Lollards formed a considerable part of the population.
In 1395 they even ventured to address a petition
to the Parliament, in which they not only repeated
Wycliffe's complaints against abuses in the Church but
laid stress upon some of the extreme views to which
their master had hardly more than reservedly given
expression. Looking then at the numbers and strength
of the Lollard party, one cannot but be surprised at the
small number of recorded cases in which they came under
official cognisance. A few persons here and there,
particularly in the diocese of Lincoln, were proceeded
against; but their punishments were for the most part
lenient. The gentleness with which the movement
was met is probably explained in some degree by the
fact that the bishops recognised the general high character and moral efficiency of the Lollard preachers,
and partly also by the extensive support which they
received from the country people and the country
gentlemen who honestly advocated their cause in the
House of Commons. In 1389, it is true, there were

*Strength of
Lollardy in
England.*

some attempts at concerted measures to repress them: the Bishop of Worcester issued a mandate directed, under the name of Lollards, against the itinerant preachers; and in the same year Archbishop Courtenay visited Leicester and excommunicated certain heretics, with the result that in ten days they all confessed their errors and were admitted to penance and absolution. But the chroniclers with one voice condemn the lukewarmness of the prelates in the cause of orthodoxy, noting only with praise that the Bishop of Norwich—the same crusading bishop whom we have met with before—effectually purged his diocese of heresy by a threat of committing Wycliffites to the flames. In 1397 indeed Archbishop Arundel held a provincial synod in which eighteen articles taken from Wycliffe's writings were condemned; but under Richard the Second he had no opportunity to carry the work further.

A turning-point arrived in the history of the reforming party at the accession of the house of Lancaster. King Henry the Fourth was not only a devoted son of the Church, but he owed his success in no slight measure to the assistance of the churchmen, and above all to that of Archbishop Arundel. It was felt that the new dynasty and the hierarchy stood or fell together. A mixture of religious and political motives led to the passing of the well-known statute 'De hæretico comburendo' in 1401, and thenceforward Lollardy was a capital offence. Lamentable as were the results of that statute, it still remains a fact that only two heretics are known to have suffered death for their opinions. Doubtless the abortive movement which was believed to be directed by Sir John Oldcastle in 1414 involved a large number of Lollards in the condemnation to which their leader was afterwards subjected; but their sentence was expressly decided not only by their guilt of heresy but also of treason.

The one statute 'De hæretico comburendo' had for the present but few victims; it did its work with success Wycliffites and very quickly, and the Lollards in a genera-
at Oxford tion ceased to be counted among the parties of English life. In Oxford alone had it been found necessary to take further resolute steps against them. Archbishop Arundel, who held a provincial council there in 1407, ordered that all books written in Wycliffe's time should pass through the censorship first of the University of Oxford or Cambridge, and secondly of the Archbishop himself, before they might be used in the schools. Two years later he risked a serious quarrel with the University in order to secure the appointment of a committee to make a list of heresies and errors to be found in Wycliffe's writings. The committee was eventually constituted, two hundred and sixty-seven propositions condemned, and the obnoxious books solemnly burned at Carfax. Not long after a copy of the list of condemned articles was ordered to be preserved in the public library, and oaths against their maintenance were enjoined upon all members of the University on graduation. Yet even these ordinances did not succeed in stamping out the academical tradition of Wycliffism. So late as 1427 we find Fleming, the Bishop of Lincoln, earnestly engaged in founding a college at Oxford with the express view of resisting the current of heresy, and even beyond the middle of

the century there are still expiring traces—if chiefly in the memory of the elder men—of that which had had so hearty a vitality in a previous generation.

But outside Oxford the Lollards had long before this time lost all the influence and position they once possessed, and the fact that they were reduced so easily and with such small expense of violence can only be accounted for on the ground that the movement they represented had spent its energy and thus that the bishops did not think it worth their while to proceed to extremity against any considerable number of them, or else that the Lollards themselves recognised the hopelessness of their cause and were ready enough to return to the communion of the Church on little compulsion. Whatever be the reason, it remains certain that from the time of Oldcastle's death in 1417 no further action was deemed necessary against the Lollards. They lived on in small numbers and in scattered congregations; but their potency for the progress of English religion or the changes of English policy was past. The day of small things has come; there is no longer a great leader, whether for good or evil, in Church or State. Towards the middle of the fifteenth century we are only, as it were, awakened to the fact that there were still Lollards in the land by the attack made on them by Bishop Reginald Pecock of Chichester, an attack made by a genuine free-thinker, which involved its author himself in a charge of heresy and in condemnation. Evidently Lollardy could not be dangerous if its foremost assailant could be brought to judgement because his method of proceeding was too liberal. That there continued a Wycliffite tradition

Decline of Lollardy.

without a break until the time of the Protestant Reformation in the sixteenth century need not be questioned; but it was so slight and attenuated that it exercised no appreciable influence upon our later religious history.

It was not on England but on Bohemia that Wycliffe's real legacy devolved. There his doctrines were eagerly planted and nourished, and grew up to form a power of decisive moment in the national history. A connexion between such distant countries as England and Bohemia was possible in the Middle Ages in a way in which it has never been possible since, thanks to the international position of the universities and the use of Latin as an international language in all concerns of education. The University of Prague recently established by the Emperor Charles the Fourth had risen in a few years into a European eminence. Founded on the models of Paris, Bologna, and Oxford, it attracted to itself, while it sent forth to other centres, the commerce of learning. In 1388 Adalbert Ranconis, a great teacher at Prague and a man himself filled with a lively zeal for Church reform, bequeathed a sum of money—for travelling scholarships, as we should say,—to assist Bohemian lads to study at Paris or Oxford; and the circumstance that King Richard the Second had in 1382 married a Bohemian queen naturally encouraged a further intercourse between the two countries, especially since Queen Anne herself was believed to be not unfriendly to the new doctrines. The Bohemian students continued to flock to England long after her death in 1394, and there are manuscripts in existence of Wycliffe's writings which were transcribed by them in remote English villages as late as the first quarter of the following century.

While thus in several ways a road was opened for the passage of Lollard opinions into Bohemia, in that Reform move- country also there had been for some time ment in Bohemia. a steady current in the direction of Church reform. Charles the Fourth, who was much more a a Bohemian king than Roman emperor, had shown unmeasured favour to the Church. He had sought anxiously to correct abuses in its organisation and moral condition, and above all to purge it of any taint of heresy. That the activity devoted to the purpose in his time was urgently needed is proved abundantly by the records of ecclesiastical visitations ; it is also clear that the attempted reform failed to produce any great change. Meanwhile a succession of whole-hearted workers set themselves to stir the Bohemian people into a conviction that it lay with them to begin a move-

Conrad of ment for the better. The first of these was Waldhausen. Conrad of Waldhausen, an Augustinian friar, who however from his German birth and speech can hardly be conceived to have spoken to the Czech people at large. He seems to have possessed the magnetic genius of the great preacher, and for years before his death, which occurred apparently in middle life in 1369, maintained an unrivalled influence in his church at Prague. Unfortunately only his Latin sermons, addressed to the students, are preserved, and these naturally cannot be taken as examples of his popular discourses. Yet they show us sufficiently the secret of the power he exercised : he was first and foremost a moral teacher, an unsparing assailant of vices and abuses wherever he found them, and he was no respecter of persons ; himself a mendicant, he denounced the failings of his brethren. But possibly his influence was chiefly notable because Conrad was not only a preacher but a master of preachers. His sermons were eagerly collected and used as models by his hearers. So extensively were they in demand that a second and briefer recension of them was circulated for general convenience.

If Conrad represents the German element in the reforming movement in Bohemia, the native Czech element is still more powerfully displayed in the work of his greater contemporary Milicz of Kremsier, archdeacon of Prague, though he also was not by birth a Bohemian but a Moravian. As strenuous as Conrad was in his moral earnestness, he surpassed him in the spiritual force of his character. He laid so great a stress upon the duties of the religious life that he was said to have denounced the study of the liberal arts as sinful. Far less did he spare the worldly vices of his day, whether they belonged to high or low. Bishops and archbishops were not free from his censure, nor even the Emperor Charles the Fourth himself. He had a peculiar doctrine concerning Antichrist which probably connects him with the Spiritual party among the Franciscans, and which led him once to point to the Emperor at a great assembly in 1366, with the declaration that he was the Antichrist. Naturally he was summoned to answer for his words before the Pope ; but he escaped with a short imprisonment at Rome. A second time he was cited, and went to Avignon in 1374, but died while he was awaiting his sentence.

Milicz of Kremsier.

Side by side with Conrad the Austrian preacher and Milicz the Moravian enthusiast, worked the Bohemian scholar Adalbert Ranconis, one of the leading furtherers of the national movement for the advancement of Bohemian religion and literature. He had been an eminent doctor at Paris, and was afterwards professor at the University of Prague and canon of the cathedral. He was a great teacher and a keen disputant; he was also busied in all the interests of his city and country, social, moral, and educational. But, free from any suspicion of incorrect opinions, he is only ranked among the forerunners of the Bohemian reformation because he stimulated life and thought in a way which in time converged with other and less orthodox tendencies. The point of union is indicated by the position of Thomas of Štitný, who was a warm friend both of Milicz and of Adalbert, correct himself in doctrine, but troubled and perplexed by the religious tumult that arose about him in the closing years of the fourteenth century.

Adalbert Ranconis.

Thomas of Štitný.

Matthias of Janow, who died in 1394, is another link, in fact he has generally been conceived to form the direct link, connecting these earlier teachers with John Hus. Such a view of his relation can hardly be maintained, since on the one hand there is no trace in him (with a single exception) of any opposition to the accepted Church system either in doctrine or organisation, and on the other there is no evidence that Hus derived any of his ideas from him. Matthias like Štitný represents the last stage in the national reform-movement, before it came into contact with foreign influences; in other words he

Matthias of Janow.

prepares the transition in Bohemian opinion which was decided in a Protestant direction by the importation of the works of Wycliffe. Personally attached both to Adalbert Ranconis and to John of Jenzenstein the Archbishop of Prague, a traveller and a Paris student, Matthias became a canon of Prague and won an influential position through his writings. With an ascetic strain of temperament, he was naturally roused to reprove sharply the existing disorders of the Church. If at one time he included among these the popular excesses of image-worship, he had no scruple in making an ample retractation when called upon in 1389. It is indeed not in any point of doctrine that he approaches the coming religious movement, but in the tone of his mind, his ardent study of the Bible, and his advocacy of preaching in the mother-tongue.

The former of these two characteristics is that which gradually becomes more and more prominent; the John of latter is conspicuous in the aims of all the Štékna. Bohemian reformers, perhaps in none more than in John of Štékna, of whom Hus speaks as 'the illustrious preacher with trumpet-voice.' But such vernacular sermons were no novelty in Bohemia; they are mentioned by Ludolf of Sagan, who lived towards the end of the fourteenth century, as a time-honoured institution. In Prague, he says, 'there was from of old a people mixed of two languages, wherefore the rectors of the churches were wont to preach in either of them, even as they thought expedient for their hearers.' But, just as in the parallel movement in England, this popular preaching furnished a means that lent itself readily to adaptation, and thus to the diffusion of the new religious views. Those new views had indeed not as yet been introduced into Bohemia; the native growth might seem only so far dangerous that it was severely critical of abuses in the Church. But the Bohemian teachers unquestionably prepared an atmosphere of feeling that at least in the public mind tended towards an antagonism to the state of religion as it then was, an atmosphere the existence of which was essential to the success of Hus's teaching a few years later.

The bringing of Wycliffe's books into Bohemia forms the decisive epoch which divides the reforming movement there into two distinct periods, and gave an entirely fresh vitality to it. The date of this importation has generally been fixed in 1406 or 1407; but it is certain that a number of Wycliffe's writings were read in Bohemia several years before this. Hus himself made a copy of some of his philosophical treatises in 1398, and about three years later Wycliffe's theological writings were carried home by Jerome of Prague on his return from studying at Oxford. The books must have been eagerly read and multiplied; the doctrine must have spread like wildfire: for in May 1403, when it had probably been known hardly more than a year in the country, it was solemnly condemned by the University of Prague. The condemnation included the twenty-four articles condemned by the Blackfriars council of 1382, as well as twenty-one others put forth as taken from Wycliffe's writings by one of the Prague masters. Hus's protest on this occasion brings him for the first

Introduction of Wycliffe's works.

time forward as a disciple of Wycliffe. Its issues belong closely to the personal history of the reformer, to which we cannot turn without reviewing the contemporary history of the Schism and the attempts to restore unity in Christendom.

CHAPTER IX.

THE DIVIDED PAPACY.

THE accident that Gregory the Eleventh died at Rome had made it necessary that the election of his suc-
The Schism 1378.
cessor should take place there ; and it was the violence of the Roman populace that had frightened the cardinals into choosing an Italian Pope. Themselves in a great majority Frenchmen, they had soon found out their mistake,—all the sooner because five months after his election Urban the Sixth had been careful to secure himself by the nomination of twenty-eight new cardinals, a number sufficient not merely to overpower but to crush the French majority
September 20.
in the college. Two days afterwards the malcontents elected their Antipope, Robert of Geneva, or Clement the Seventh.[1] Thus began the great Schism in the Church, which undermined its spiritual position and influence in a way that no previous rupture or contest had weakened it. Empe-

---

[1] It is hardly necessary to mention that as the line of popes commenced by Clement was ultimately deposed by the Council of Constance, these Popes are not reckoned as Catholic. Hence we have the inconvenience of the repetition of the style ' Clement the Seventh,' borne also by the Pope with whom King Henry the Eighth negotiated for his divorce.

rors before this had often withstood the Pope, and set
up a rival bishop; but such resistance generally left
the Pope who was assailed only stronger than before.
Now it was the action of the cardinals themselves
that broke up the unity of the Church; and for a
generation to come we find the acceptance of one pope
or the other to be a mere matter of national policy in
this or that country. Universal councils are held to
decide between the claimants; at first they only add
to the confusion. Then Christendom thus assembled
declares its power to set aside the opposing candidates,
to proclaim the holy See vacant, and to appoint a
lawful Pope. Even now it is long before peace is
finally restored to the Church. A strain of feeling
had been aroused, a sense of dissatisfaction with the
existing state of things, which might be appeased for
a while, but could not be extinguished. It is, in fact,
from the days of the schism that it becomes more and
more evident that a great religious change is at hand
in Western Europe; and it was the cardinals at Rome
in 1378 who laid the foundation of the movement
which culminated in the religious revolt of the sixteenth century.

If the spectacle of two pontiffs dividing between
them the outward allegiance of Latin Christendom was
humiliating to all true churchmen, still less was their
discontent likely to be softened by the contemplation
of the personal character of their champions. Urban
the Sixth was a man of little cultivation of mind, of
brutal manners, who could act when he pleased, and
he often pleased, with the ferocity of a barbarian.
Clement might not be less cruel by nature, but his

cruelty was so evidently directed by policy that it
seemed rather to enhance the opinion men were ready
to form of his firmness and resolution, while his address and courtesy marked him as one designed to
play a part in affairs requiring the delicate judgement of a man of the world. In both alike the
moral element is the least conspicuous, and we
should seek long before we discovered a trace of it
in the public career of either. Christendom looked on
helplessly, depressed by the scandal, and yet impotent to remove it. The kingdoms of Europe were
hardly one of them in a position to exercise effective
pressure. At the time of the schism England had
been for a year past governed by a boy ; France was
shortly to pass under the rule of another, who grew
up to be a maniac ; while in Germany, a few months
after the schism broke out, Charles the Fourth died,
and was succeeded by his son, the drunken Wenzel ;
Naples, always a disturbing force in Italian politics,
was now during the last years of Queen Joan the
First divided among the factions that strove for her
inheritance. Each Pope took sides in the affair.
Queen Joan, after many fruitless arrangements, at
length adopted Lewis of Anjou, brother to the French
king, as her successor ; and Lewis as the French can-
didate was as a matter of course supported by Clement,
who even invested him with a new kingdom, that of
Adria, consisting of the greater part of the estates of
the Church. Living himself under the shadow of
France he took no interest in Italy save as a means
towards advancing his own cause. Urban, on the
other hand, moved from place to place in the land,

making himself daily more unpopular, and bent chiefly
on the establishment of his nephew Francesco Prignano,
better known as Butillo, in a commanding position;
but the superfluity of naughtiness in which Butillo
revelled only increased his uncle's difficulties. The
cardinals in his train sought to put some check on the
Pope's excesses, and were rewarded by imprisonment
and repeated tortures; after a time five of them were
secretly murdered by Urban's command.

In the midst of all this tumult and fury Urban was
ceaselessly engaged in the task of conquering the
allegiance of those who upheld his rival. The ' Clementines ' must be opposed by arms, and crusades were
set on foot with a profuse expenditure of indulgences.
In 1383 England, so long excited by military enter-
prises, entered eagerly into the religious expedition to
Flanders, headed by Henry Despenser, Bishop of Norwich, but less because it was enjoined by the Pope
than because it was an attack upon France and the
dependants of France. The failure of the campaign
did not prevent the expedient being repeated; and
when John of Gaunt joined the King of Portugal, who
stood by Urban, in an attack upon Castile, this also
became a crusade and was promoted by such lavish
bulls of indulgences as to inspire amazement, if not
disgust, in the minds of sober men. Doubtless in thus
arousing and playing upon the adventurous instincts
of Englishmen Urban was influenced by the fact that
it was from England that he drew his principal means
of support : to keep her employed in his service was
the most likely way of sustaining his interests. But
the whole history of the devices he adopted is a preg-

nant satire on the character which the head of the
Church assumed ; and while Urban preyed upon England, Clement made as industrious, if less productive,
ravages upon France. In 1389, a few months before
the jubilee from which he expected a rich harvest,
Urban died at Rome, and his line was continued by the
election of a Neapolitan cardinal, Boniface the Ninth.

The longer the schism lasted the more impracticable
did it appear to heal it, and still the more necessary
Suggestions
for reunion. was it that action should be taken. Three
chief proposals gradually formed themselves.
Either a general council should be summoned with full
powers to deal with the rival claims ; or the claims
should be submitted to arbitration ; or each Pope should
abdicate, either to his own college of cardinals, or to a
joint body of the two colleges of the two Popes. The
first of these alternatives, though the earliest to be suggested, was not at first pressed ; the second was seen
to labour under the decisive objection, that it would
be hardly possible to enforce the arbitrator's award ;
while the third was exposed to the double disadvantage
that, however eager a Pope might profess himself to
promote union, he could never admit the possibility
that he was not the lawful Pope, and that in like
manner neither Pope could admit the legitimacy of the
college of cardinals created by his rival. The one Pope
and his college must of necessity regard the other Pope
and his college as schismatical. The very sublimity
of the pretensions of the Papacy took it out of the
cognisance of earthly arbitration or jurisdiction. On
the other hand the splendour of these pretensions, however essential they might appear to the Pope himself,

had been so rudely shattered by the shock of the schism
that it now seemed more possible to deal with them.
Apart from personal considerations which might alienate men's feelings—the cupidity, the meanness, the self-
seeking of the Popes,—the great idea of the unity of
Christendom had been broken, and this must be restored at whatever expense.

The University of Paris was foremost in taking
measures to promote this end. Pope Boniface so far
entered into them that he opened negotiations with Charles the Sixth; but his motive
was simply to endeavour to win back France
from his rival. The proposals of the University containing the three alternative suggestions above mentioned were favourably treated by the King; and by his
order they were sent on to Avignon, where the cardinals
were induced to confess that there was no choice but
to accept some one of the schemes proposed. Clement
soon after died of apoplexy, and the cardinals
forthwith elected Peter de Luna, a Spanish
cardinal, who took the title of Benedict the Thirteenth.
The choice and the circumstances were alike significant; for the new Pope had been the most powerful of
Clement's counsellors and was deemed the most resolute
against any compromise with the Italian Pope. To
this end he had laboured, and he had his reward. But
besides this, at the moment the cardinals were engaged
in his election, messengers from France were on their
way to Avignon urging that no step should be taken
without further consideration. The King and the
University each sent their advice, but Benedict was
already elected. He had however solemnly under-

Action of the
University of
Paris.

Sept. 16, 1394.

taken to do all he could to end the schism, even though
he were required to abdicate; and this proviso was
gladly seized by those who were earnest in the matter
as giving an opening to steps of a practical kind.
The University of Paris advised that both Popes should
resign. Its judgement was read in February 1395 before a national council in the capital, and was sustained
by a majority of about four to one. A mission, headed
by the Dukes of Burgundy, Berry, and Orleans, proceeded to Avignon to lay before Pope Benedict the
various schemes that had been proposed and to urge
him to abdicate. The cardinals appeared not unfavourable; but the Pope stood firm, and his strenuous resistance to every proposal in detail rendered the negotiation fruitless.

The long interchange of schemes that followed
has its importance because it served to prepare public
opinion for a more penetrating reform than the mere
removal of the existing occupants of the Papal throne,
and brought into conspicuous notice the views and
aims of men like Jean Gerson and Pierre d'Ailly,
who were destined to exercise so profound an influence
upon the later developments of the ecclesiastical history
of their time. Nor was it only at Paris that the question was agitated. Other universities were also consulted, and Oxford and Toulouse gave their decision in
favour of the summons of a general council to decide
the matter. It was afterwards seen that they had
judged rightly, that their scheme was the only prac-
ticable one. But for the moment the alternative of
abdication was more popular. It was accepted by
Richard the Second, as well as by the King of France,

who solemnly agreed to it at a meeting which he had at Rheims with Wenzel in March 1398. The three leading princes of Western Europe were thus in accord as to the principle on which the difficulty should be adjusted. Pierre d'Ailly, who was now Bishop of Cambray, was despatched to the courts of Rome and Avignon with a charge to announce the resolution ; but the mission was ineffectual, since each Pope without absolutely rejecting the proposal insisted that his rival should set the example of abdicating.

While these negotiations were going on, a national council was held in Paris. It was summoned by the Renunciation of Benedict XIII. 1398. royal command in May, and after long debate it determined to renounce allegiance to Benedict the Thirteenth : this resolution was ratified by the King in the following July. Benedict thus lost the support, above all the pecuniary support, upon which he depended from France. The Marshal Boucicault was next sent to Avignon with an armed force to compel the Pope's submission ; and Benedict after a long siege accepted terms by which he was left a partial prisoner in the hands of the citizens of Avignon. In this state he continued for nearly four years, until March 1403, when he made his escape. But in the meanwhile several things had occurred which tended in his favour, or at least removed elements which stood in the way of his recognition. The English and the German King had each been deposed ; and in France Pope Benedict had found a protector in the Duke of Orleans. He had thus the benefit of a partial reaction ; and soon after his escape a national assembly was held at Paris in which the Orleanist party secured

the acknowledgement of his title, subject to an engagement on his part to resign in the event of Boniface's
abdication, deposition, or death.

In little more than a year such an opportunity occurred. Boniface, who had spent his energies on two
main objects, the making provision for his friends and
the securing of his temporal power in Rome and the
Estates of the Church (in which latter aim he achieved
a remarkable success), died on the 1st October 1404;
but such was the tumultuous condition of Rome and
such the peril from without, that the cardinals had
hardly a choice but to proceed at once to the election
of a new Pope. They took an oath that whoever
should be made Pope would abdicate if necessary in
the interest of the restoration of union; and a Neapolitan cardinal was elected, who took the name of
Innocent the Seventh. Negotiations were promptly
resumed between the two Popes. Benedict started
from Avignon, in order, as he professed, to come to
terms with Innocent. He travelled leisurely until in
a year's time he reached Savona. But he soon found
he was in danger of losing his support from France.
The University of Paris was still active in debating
the great problem of restoring union; it again raised
the question of withdrawing obedience from Benedict.
The matter was referred by the King's council to the
Parliament which met in June 1406, and the result
of a long discussion was to declare in set terms ' that
the Gallican Church should remain thenceforth and
for ever free from the services, tithes, procurations,
and other additional subventions unduly introduced
by the Roman Church.' The national element was

again about to play its part in the relations between France and the Papacy, and a synod was appointed to meet in the following November to consider the pressing scandal of the schism.

But before the synod met Innocent the Seventh was dead. A hope arose once again that the favourable moment had come, and that Christendom would now be rescued from the evil of division. But the blind haste of the Roman cardinals disappointed all such expectations. They elected, however, one who was believed to be in accord with the universal desire for reunion, and openly chose him for that reason. They also tied his hands by prohibiting the creation of any more cardinals for a period of fifteen months. The new Pope was an aged and respected Venetian, Angelo Correr, who was crowned under the title of Gregory the Twelfth. He soon moved northward, to Viterbo and Siena, in order to have the promised conference with Benedict. He was at Lucca by January 1408. But as he drew nearer to Savona the difficulties of the situation appeared to him, a man now of past eighty years of age, unsurmountable. He sought to change the time or the place of meeting, and trust to the kindness of fortune.

Rome was now in the hands of King Ladislas of Naples. Danger seemed to lie both before and behind the anxious Pope. Thinking to gain strength he created four cardinals, an act which was naturally understood as proof of his insincerity and which hastened a crisis that led irresistibly to his own downfall. The old cardinals repudiated their new colleagues and with-

Gregory XII.

Dec. 5, 1406.

April 1408.

The crisis precipitated.

drew to Pisa, where they published their appeal from
Pope Gregory to a general council.

If Benedict's opportunity had now come, he did not
know how to make use of it.   But in truth difficulties
were rising about him not less serious than those
which encompassed Gregory.   In the previous November Benedict had lost his main advocate in France by
the murder of the Duke of Orleans, whose removal
had given free room again for the University of Paris
to move and work in.   It now roused the King to
announce formally to the Pope that until one Pope
was acknowledged by Christendom France withdrew
her obedience from both claimants.   Benedict was
ready with his answer: he had written a bull, dated
months back but never promulgated, in which all who
resisted the Pope and cardinals by renunciation or appeal
were declared excommunicate ; and that bull he now
despatched to the King.   It was as fatal a step to him as
the creation of the cardinals was to Gregory.   The University of Paris pronounced the bull to be a flagrant
invasion of the dignity of the French crown and nation,
and it was publicly destroyed with contumely.   Benedict's interests at Paris received a blow from which
they never recovered ; and the Pope had no choice but
to flee to Spanish ground, where he might feel at least
personally independent both of France and Italy.   So
to Perpignan he retreated, and there in November
1408 he held a council which was intended as a
counter-manifesto to that summoned by the cardinals
at Pisa for the following March.   In like manner—to
anticipate for a moment the order of events—just
as the Council of Pisa was closing its deliberations,

Gregory also held his council at Cividale in the Gulf of Venice, a council more poorly attended and more inconclusive than that of Benedict. Both Popes seemed bent on ending their reigns in melodrama; and by this time the Council of Pisa had added a third claimant to the obedience of Christendom.

CHAPTER X.

THE COUNCILS OF PISA AND CONSTANCE.

THE importance of the Council of Pisa lies in the fact
that it recognised, for the first time since the great
Position of the development of the Papal power, the neces-
Council of Pisa. sity of subjecting it to some definite limitations.   Hitherto there had been no redress against
an incompetent or disreputable Pope.   Often indeed
the secular estate, as represented by the Emperor or
more recently by the King of France, had stepped in
to protest against the actions of a Pope, or even to
declare his deposition and appoint another Pope in his
room.   But the mere fact that such proceedings had
originated from secular persons, however largely they
might be supported by the clergy, prevented them
from receiving universal acknowledgement.   They invariably failed of more than a momentary success, because they were felt as an intrusion by the laity upon
the domain of the Church; they appeared dangerous,
even sacrilegious.   Now however it was the cardinals
themselves who by the summons of the Council of Pisa
opened the case against the rival Popes; as indeed upon
them that duty lay with peculiar weight, since it was the
cardinals—their own predecessors in title—who were

directly responsible, as we have seen, for the existence of the schism. Had they borne with Urban the Sixth, hard though it were, and not ventured upon the perilous innovation of setting up Clement the Seventh in opposition to him, the schism and its far-reaching consequences might have been avoided. Other Popes with even less claim than Urban to the allegiance of Christian men had been endured ; and it was the mere partisanship of the French faction in the college that brought this great evil upon Europe.

But, an evil though it was, the schism had at all events taught men to look facts in the face and clear Ripening of their minds of a good many notions which opinion at it. though not a part of ancient tradition were still old enough to have acquired the dignity of axiomatic truth. We perceive the rapidity with which in a single generation opinion had moved towards the position of Wycliffe with regard to Church politics, when an accredited exponent of Church principles, Pierre d'Ailly, could declare without offence, just before the meeting of the council, what was precisely Wycliffe's own doctrine respecting the Church : ' The head of the Church,' he said, ' is Christ ; and the unity of the Church consists in union with him and not in union with any particular Pope.' Right though it was that the Papal power should be organised as the regular machinery for the government of the Church, still the original authority remained with the Church catholic, which in case of need was bound to exercise it for the common good of Christendom. A general council to carry out such a purpose might be summoned by the cardinals, and not by them merely but by any faithful men who were in a position to secure its efficiency. The council might call upon the rival Popes to defend themselves and, if they refused, might take proceedings against them as schismatical; while in the last resort it was empowered to make a new election, provided only that it felt sure of the support of the Catholic world.

Such were the views with reference to the power of the ecumenical council expressed by Ailly. Their correspondence with Wycliffe's doctrine, especially considering that it is quite unlikely that their propounder was at all acquainted with the English reformer's writings, is but another evidence of the way in which opinions that had hitherto been discussed by scholars in a speculative manner had now passed into the common currency of religious men and had come to furnish the motive-power by which the Council of Pisa acted, or at least upon which it depended for popular support. Yet if the council had (to use a modern phrase) to appeal to the constituencies, its practical procedure was guided by less generous and more worldly principles; and the man who controlled its deliberations and gave them their definitive form was one who simply worked for his own aggrandisement, the famous or infamous Baldassare Cossa, destined very soon to become Pope and in not many years to be deposed with ignominy by a far more powerful and more representative council than that which met at Pisa.

The council summoned by the cardinals met on the morrow of Lady Day 1409. Besides twenty-two cardinals belonging to both colleges, there were present either in person or by proxies two hundred arch-

bishops and bishops, and nearly as many abbots; representatives of the religious orders and chapters, of the
Meeting of the kings and great princes of Europe (those
Council of Pisa. of Spain being conspicuously absent), and
of eleven universities; together with a multitude of
doctors of theology, making up a total not far short of
a thousand members. At the first session of this imposing assembly the two Popes were cited, and on their
non-appearance it was agreed that after a fair interval
they should be pronounced contumacious. Considerable discussion took place during this interval; opposition was aroused, and the term was prolonged.
At length on the 25th May Gregory and Benedict
Deposition of were declared guilty of contumacy, and on
the Popes. the 5th June they were solemnly deposed.
Only then did the ambassadors of Pope Benedict make
their appearance, and in spite of the appeal of the
King of Aragon the council declined to hear them : it
had empowered the cardinals to elect a new Pope, and
they were now about to enter conclave. Their natural
choice would have fallen on Baldassare Cossa, but he
besought them earnestly to pass him by. They were
resolved however not to bind themselves for too long
Election of a time, and so chose a man past seventy years
Alexander V. of age, highly esteemed for learning and
liberality, Peter Philargi, who as a Greek might be
accepted as a convenient compromise at a time when
the Pope's nationality had so long been an incentive
to division. This done, the council felt it had exerted
itself sufficiently; the questions of Church reform which
stood as part of their business were hardly touched, but
a new council was promised for April 1412. Then on the

7th August the fathers of Pisa dissolved their sessions,
congratulating themselves on having restored unity to
Christendom, when they had in fact only added one
more to the rival claimants of the Papal See.   The
council had placed itself too entirely in the hands of
the cardinals, and had been too abrupt in its dealings
with Benedict and Gregory.   It assumed the validity
of its own position and declined to enter into the
difficulty of theirs.   Some years more of negotiation
and conflict were needed before the purpose for which
the Council of Pisa strove ineffectually could be secured
by the Council of Constance.

The Pope who owed his election to the council, Alexander the Fifth, lived less than a year; and his pontificate
is only noticeable for the support which, as a
Franciscan, he gave to his order, in such a
way as to arouse all the antagonistic forces of the University of Paris, and for the vigorous proceedings of
his legate Cossa in Italy, which ended just before he
died in the recovery of the city of Rome.   Cossa, it was
seen, was the one man who would succeed him, if the
third line of Popes was to be continued with any
vitality.   His energy in conducting affairs that called
for despatch and resolution was a conspicuous merit,
and his steady hostility to the encroachments of Ladislas of Naples was felt to be so valuable a qualification
as to outweigh any compunction that might be excited
by his notoriously bad private character.   He maintained through life the notions of honourable dealing
that he had learned in his early apprenticeship as a
pirate.   Perfectly unscrupulous and profligate to a
degree that shocked even Italy in his age, the pressing

John XXIII.
1410.

need of a strong defender against Naples decided his election, and on the 16th May 1410 he became Pope under the name of John the Twenty-third. But the hopes that he would overcome Ladislas were soon disappointed, for though he defeated him a year later the victory was worse than fruitless. The Neapolitan power grew in strength until in June 1411 it was able to impose terms of peace upon the Pope, who acknowledged Ladislas as King of the Two Sicilies—though the island belonged to Aragon—on the sole condition that he would bring pressure to bear upon Gregory the Twelfth to induce him to abdicate.

The council announced by that of Pisa to be held in the spring of 1412 was actually held at Rome in February 1413. The one act for which it is remembered is the condemnation of Wycliffe's writings which was decreed on the 13th February and forthwith carried out by a solemn burning of the books on the steps of St. Peter's. But what made a deeper impression upon those present at vespers in the Pope's chapel just before the first session of the council, was the appearance of an owl which, when the Holy Spirit was invoked, came and settled upon the Pope's head. The significance of so sinister a portent could not be mistaken. At the council itself the attendance was so thin, and the members were so certain that the presiding forces at it were not in earnest in the matter of reform, that it broke up of itself without being formally dissolved. On the 3rd March John the Twenty-third summoned another which should meet in the following December,—where, was to be fixed hereafter. John, it may be affirmed, had no idea of fulfilling this

Council at Rome, 1413.

engagement; but fortune steadily drove him towards
it.   The King of Naples moved against him, in June
took Rome by surprise : the Pope fled to Viterbo, to
Florence, then into Lombardy.   Here at Cremona in
December he met the German King Sigismund, who
arranged to treat with his ambassadors about the choice
of the place where the council should be held, and succeeded in persuading them to procure a proclamation
of it fixed for November of the following
Dec. 9, 1413.   year, and in the imperial city of Constance.
To Popes Gregory and Benedict and to the Kings of
France (still the mad Charles the Sixth) and Aragon
Sigismund addressed his own summons.   ' Once more
the old imperial pretensions were revived, and the rule
of Christendom, by the joint action of the temporal and
spiritual power was set forward.' [1]

By the following autumn Ladislas was dead and
Rome safe in the Pope's hands ; his alliance with Sigismund might seem to have been but a vain extravagance, since without it he might now feel secure at
home, while with it he was compelled to submit to the
doubtful guidance—to him, as it proved, the doom—
of the coming council.   He had joined Sigismund for
political reasons, and found that the alliance bound him
to a man who was pledged with his whole heart to the
truly imperial design of restoring union to Christendom.   Little as John desired the prospect, there was
now no help for it, and to Constance he needs must go.
In October 1414, a few days before Rome was officially
occupied by his legate in his name, he set out on the

[1] Creighton, *History of the Papacy,* I. 253.

last stage of his journey, through Verona and Trent, reaching Constance before the end of the month.

The council which John the Twenty-third declared to be a continuation and completion of that of Pisa The Council of was formally opened on the 5th November. Constance, 1414. At first it looked almost like a mere synod of Italian dignitaries ; but as the numbers swelled it soon became evident that as little could its work be limited by the interests of the cardinals or any national Church, as could its design be restricted to the final establishment of unity in the head of Christendom. Unity had been nominally secured by the Council of Pisa ; and yet Benedict the Thirteenth was still vigorous in Spain, while Gregory the Twelfth was by no means abandoned in Italy. That the successor of the Pope created by the Council of Pisa had the largest following in Europe was a fact that depended entirely upon his recognition of the principle that a general council was plenipotentiary, that it possessed the *plenitudo potestatis* which had for generations been claimed by the Pope. Yet, as we have said, John's acceptance was by no means universal, and to this extent the Council of Pisa had failed. It had failed through the flaw in its convocation, since it had been called simply by the cardinals. There was at least an equal chance that the Council of Constance would fail, in consequence of its summons by one whose title depended upon the validity of the acts of the Council of Pisa. If Pope John could only be maintained by the recognition of the supreme authority of a council, it was evident that this authority must be not only asserted but solemnly confirmed by the undoubted voice of Christendom. But Chris-

C. H. K

tendom would not be satisfied by a council summoned
merely in order to establish the title of a Pope; its
functions must extend to a wide-reaching reform of
the whole Church system. That such a reform was
not effected is not irreconcilable with the prominence
which it occupied in the minds of those who attended
the council. The question of reform was an essential
element in the proceedings, probably it was the essential element which made the ecumenical composition
of the council possible. The existence of heresy was
a symptom of the need of reform even more forcible
than the existence of the schism ; and reform was
given the first place, to which the not less necessary
measures for the restoration of unity and the suppres-
sion of heresy were ancillary and supplemental.

Before the council had fairly set to business the
Italians in a select congregation offered a proposal
that the Council of Pisa should be formally
December 7.   recognised and that a general council should
for the future be held every ten years. Reform was
just glanced at, and it was suggested that Gregory and
Benedict should be persuaded, or if necessary coerced
to abdicate. After these preliminary proposals a general congregation was held, in which Ailly maintained
that the council would lose in credit by following the
precedent of the Council of Pisa in its rigorous attitude
towards the Popes. The Council of Pisa, he urged, was
valid, since it was believed to represent the Church
Catholic, which must be supreme over all its members ;
but he added, much as Ockham had declared nearly a
century earlier, that even a general council did not
necessarily reflect truly the voice of Christendom. Even

as the Pope had erred, so the council might err. The council served as a working instrument for embodying the faith of Christendom so long as its decrees were in accord with those of the Church universal. Decision upon these declarations of principle was postponed until the arrival of Sigismund, which was on Christmas Day. But it was not until the beginning of March that the second session of the council was held. By this time the attendance at Constance had grown to an overpowering multitude. The actual members of the council exceeded five thousand persons, and the number of visitors was computed at a total not far short of a hundred thousand.

In the interval before the second session, it became evident that Sigismund was at one with Ailly upon the vital point that reform must accompany, as it was essential to, unity in the Church. The ambassadors of Popes Gregory and Benedict were received with the honour due to cardinals, and the question whether Pope John should preside when their claims were considered was openly discussed. It was arranged also that the council should divide itself into nations, in order to obviate what would otherwise have been an unfair preponderance of Italians. The council was therefore to vote by its four nations, Italian, German, French, and English. The nations debated separately, and after consultation brought forward their proposals before a general congregation of the four, whose results were to be ratified by the council in formal session. The effect of this division in hastening the moulding of opinion was seen as early as the 16th February, when all but the

1415.
Quesion of the order of business.

Division into nations.

Italian nation recommended that John the Twenty-third should abdicate in order to leave the course open for the council.   John protested his readiness to resign, but it was some time before he could be brought to fulfil his promise.   On the 1st March however he solemnly undertook to abdicate when Gregory and Benedict should do likewise.

Matters had not indeed advanced very far when the success of the council was made to depend upon the self-sacrifice of three separate persons, one of whom was the inflexible Benedict and another the unscrupulous John ; and the disputes that soon arose between Sigismund and the French rendered it likely that a little patience on the part of those principally affected by the proposed settlement would allow them to see the council gradually break up under the pressure of the conflicting forces within it.   But John, as though bent on his own destruction, precipitated matters by fleeing from Constance on the 20th March, and establishing himself at Schaffhausen. Six days later the council unanimously agreed that the Pope's withdrawal did not dissolve the council, that its business was to go on until its work was finished. Before the end of the month John, contenting himself with a protest against the validity of the council, had retired to Laufenburg lower down the Rhine ; and on the 30th, at its fourth session, the council solemnly declared its independence of the Pope, and even its supremacy over the Papal office.

Flight of John XXIII.

But the cardinals, who now saw that the reform which the council contemplated closely touched their own interests and might be ruinous to their future

position, resolved to delay the final decision by negotiations and an infinity of discussions which kept the
council busy for the next two months. By the middle
of May a series of articles was drawn up detailing the
crimes of which John the Twenty-third was guilty, as
a man, as a priest, and as Pope. Few men's lives
could have borne a close scrutiny worse than his, and
the indictment, setting aside its rancorous tone, was
a terrible one. The articles once laid before it, the
council, even had its majority been favourable to John,
could not for very shame hesitate what course to pur-
sue. On the 29th the Pope was formally deposed; he
His deposi-   had already been captured and kept under
tion.   guard; henceforth, so long as the council
sat, Baldassare Cossa was held a prisoner at Heidelberg
in the charge of the Count Palatine. While setting
aside John the Twenty-third, the council had been
careful to bind itself that it would recognise none of
the existing Popes and that no new election should
take place without its sanction.

The Council of Pisa had set aside two Popes and yet
was not able to ensure their universal repudiation; it
had only raised up a new one. His successor was now
deposed by the Council of Constance, and still the two
old rivals maintained, partially, it is true, but still maintained their ground; and the only hope lay in the general belief that the second council would be able to give,
what the first had failed to give, a real effect to their
decisions. But before a new Pope was chosen, a course
of action had been brought to completion which has
made the Council of Constance more famous than if its
deliberations had been solely devoted to the restoration

of unity in the head of Christendom. It had entered upon the other part of its scheme which pledged it to the overthrow of heresy; and six weeks after the deposition of John the Twenty-third saw the condemnation and death of John Hus.

CHAPTER XI.

JOHN HUS.

JOHN OF HUSINEÇ [1] or Hus is said to have been born in the year 1369, or more probably a few years earlier. Accustomed to the privations of a poor home, he was led to prepare himself to become a priest, seeing, as he afterwards confessed, the comfort in which the clergy lived. As a matter of course he passed on into the University of Prague, and there without gaining special distinction as a student he obtained the immense advantage of listening to teachers whose influence by degrees changed entirely his manner of thought. Among these were some who afterwards ranked among his chief enemies, such as Stanislas of Znaim and Stephen of Palecz. In 1393 he became Bachelor of Arts and in the following year of Theology; in 1396 he incepted as Master of Arts, but never proceeded to the degree of Doctor in Theology. In 1401 he was Dean of the philosophical faculty, and next year Rector of the University. His University career was thus, like all his life, unpretentious but honourable. He had won the respect of his fellow-scholars without making his mark by any startling achievement.

Hus at Prague.

[1] I venture to depart from the practice of Czech writers in indicating the softness of the letter *c* by a cedilla.

Some time before his election to the Rectorship, which he held but half a year, he had been engaged not only as a lecturer in the University, but also in active clerical work. In 1400 he had been ordained priest, and two years later was appointed preacher at the Bethlehem Chapel at Prague, an office which required him to deliver sermons in the Czech language. At the University he had known Wycliffe's His study of philosophical treatises, some of which, copied Wycliffe. out by his own hand, are still preserved ; and probably while he was Rector he made the acquaintance of the Englishman's theological writings, which, as we have already noticed,[1] had early passed into Bohemia. These almost in a moment gave rise to eager controversy among the students and teachers at Prague, and soon came to form the groundwork of a religious movement in that country of a far deeper, more general, and more abiding character than was the case in England. But Hus's studies in Wycliffe did not make him the less a devoted son of the Church. He respected his English master, and when Wycliffe's doctrines were examined by the University of Prague, made his protest—it seems mistakenly—against the correctness of the passages stated to have been extracted from Wycliffe's writings. The doctrines were condemned by the majority ; and thenceforth 'Wiclefy' became a burning party question in the University. In 1407 or 1408 two Bohemian students, Nicolas Faulfisch and George of Kniehnicz, brought back to Prague from Oxford, together with works of Wycliffe —one with their colophon is extant—a testimonial

---

[1] Above, pp. 119, 124.

bearing the seal of the University of Oxford and declaring the correctness of Wycliffe's teaching. The document was almost certainly a forgery, though the bringers of it were quite innocent of the fraud; but it aroused a good deal of excitement at Prague, and Hus, having no doubts of its genuineness, gladly availed himself of it as a vindication of his own discipleship.

All this time Hus had been rapidly making his way into the hearts of the Bohemian people. They *His popu-* listened to his discourses with a conviction *larity as a* that answers to an absolute sincerity and *preacher.* single-mindedness on the part of the preacher. And Hus's mind became more and more under the dominion of Wycliffe's teaching. He was not content with moving the religious sentiment of his hearers; he must denounce the evils in the Church at large. For a time his efforts were viewed with favour by Zbynek, the Archbishop of Prague, a worthy and well-meaning, if somewhat illiterate, prelate, who asked him to report to him any evils that came before his notice in the Church. Through the same influence Hus appears in 1405 as preacher to the annual synod, in which quality he did not spare the vices and disorders which he saw in the lives and conversation of the clergy. But by 1407 the Archbishop had come to feel that Hus was going too far, or at least too fast. He had already been warned by Innocent the Seventh in 1405 of the necessity under which he lay of uprooting Wycliffism in his province; and when in 1408 the *Opposition of* clergy of his diocese addressed him a me- *the clergy.* morial against Hus, on account of the attack, as they considered it, which he had made upon themselves in his last synodal sermon, Zbynek could not but connect his actions with the danger which it was his duty to resist. Hus therefore was deprived of the office of preaching before the synod, but in other respects he was left as before. On the 20th May the Archbishop repeated the former condemnation of the Wycliffite articles, but the Bohemian nation in the University so modified the condemnation when urged upon them as to show that they were not prepared to admit that Wycliffe's doctrine as such was heretical.

The Bohemian nation was soon however to take up a more resolute position with regard to the chief questions at that time agitated in the Church. In 1408, when the Council of Pisa was already summoned by the cardinals, King Wenzel of Bohemia (he was no longer King of the Romans) renounced his obedience to Pope Gregory the Twelfth, and sought to obtain the support of his own clergy and University for an attitude of neutrality towards the rival Popes. The Archbishop of Prague however declined to follow him, and of the four nations at Prague only the Bohemian agreed to be neutral; the other three stood by Gregory. They were also parted by the old scholastic feud; the Bohemians were realists, while the others were nominalists. The Bohemians thought that they might use the opportunity for establishing the predominance of their nation in the University. They requested Wenzel to grant them three votes to the single one of the foreign nations. Hus was an ardent advocate of the change. It became a national question between the Czech and the other elements in the University, and on the 19th

January 1409 the King—willingly enough, we may believe—issued the required decree.

It is seldom that a mere academical ordinance is a matter of the first importance in the history of a people ; but the decree which placed the Czechs in a position of command at the University of Prague formed a very real landmark in that of Bohemia. A multitude of scholars, estimated variously at between two and twenty thousand—in any case a considerable proportion of the total number of masters and students,—quitted Prague, and went forth to found or to invigorate the Universities of Vienna, Leipzig, and Cologne. At Leipzig the building now occupied by the philosophical faculty is the very house bought by the Prague scholars on their first arrival to make the beginning of a famous seat of learning. The old University lost in a moment its international position and its high distinction among the schools of Europe. But this very fact was favourable to the development of a purely Bohemian current of opinion there ; and as Hus had been through all these proceedings the leader of the 'patriotic' party, it was almost inevitable that this should become identified with his teaching. And with the departure of the foreign masters and students the strength of the national spirit of the Bohemian University steadily increased.

Secession of the foreigners from Prague,

leaving the University strongly Hussite.

The Archbishop of Prague however had no choice but to place himself in opposition to this current of feeling. In the autumn of this same year he was persuaded to acknowledge Alexander the Fifth, and having so acknowledged him he was

1409.

bound to carry out that Pope's bull of December 20,
ordering him to suppress the writings and influence

The Arch-
bishop's ac-
tion against
Wycliffism.

of Wycliffe in Bohemia; even though he
had a year earlier publicly declared that
he had already succeeded in destroying
heresy and that there were no longer any heretics
in his diocese.   A commission was appointed,

1410.

seventeen works of Wycliffe were named as
open to objection, and all copies of them were ordered
by the Archbishop to be burned, while preaching in
any unauthorised place was interdicted.   On the 21st
June the University of Prague solemnly protested
against this ordinance; Hus and some other members
of it appealed to John the Twenty-third: but on the
16th July the books were burned, the number of
volumes collected for the purpose being more than two
hundred.   A surer proof of the popularity of Wycliffe's
teaching could not be desired; and the result of the
act of Zbynek was at once to connect Bohemian
patriotism still more closely, and now indissolubly,
with Wycliffism and with the personal guidance of
Hus.

The first measure led necessarily to a second, and
two days after the burning of the books Hus was pro-

Excommunica-
tion of Hus.

nounced excommunicate, in company with
all those who had not surrendered their
copies of Wycliffe's works.   Hus was now more than
ever the popular hero; whoever ventured to say a word
against him or against Wycliffism was apt to be
roughly handled by the citizens of Prague; and the
Archbishop became the subject of ribald satirical verses.
Hus preached all the more vigorously against the per-

secution of the memory of a teacher whom, though he did not follow him in all points, he revered as one who had given the motive-power to his own life. King Wenzel himself did his best to help him, and wrote to Pope John the Twenty-third maintaining that there was no heresy in Bohemia, and requesting him to annul the late proceedings. It is curious that in the interval Pope John had appointed four cardinals to examine Zbynek's action, and they had reported that he was not justified in ordering Wycliffe's books to be burned. Zbynek's friends however demanded a new inquiry, and this was conducted by Cardinal Oddo Colonna, the future Pope Martin the Fifth, who decided firmly in the Archbishop's favour. Soon after this King Wenzel's letter was despatched, together with others from influential persons in Bohemia. But in the circumstances there was evidently no choice but to carry out the judgement of Cardinal Oddo, who cited Hus to appear at Rome and defend himself. Hus *February 1411.* did not himself go, but sent three proctors; their arguments were judged unsatisfactory; and Hus was again excommunicated.

But John the Twenty-third found that the uncertainty of his title made it advisable to limit the sphere of opposition. There was a dispute, as it *Attitude of John XXIII.* was, in Germany as to the recent election of the King of the Romans. Sigismund of Brandenburg and Jobst of Moravia both claimed the title, while Wenzel had never acquiesced in the act of 1400 which deposed him. The Moravian claimant died, it is true, in January 1411, but Sigismund's acknowledgement was not secured until July; and much

depended on the question whether Sigismund would
recognise John as Pope. Besides, if the latter drove
Wenzel to extremities, there was a risk that he might
transfer his allegiance to Gregory the Twelfth. John's
interest therefore required that he should treat the
Bohemian question in a generous spirit ; and, thanks
doubtless to his mediation, the stress of feeling in that
country became gradually calmer. The King had at
first adopted some severe measures against Zbynek
and the Church, and Hus had come to Wenzel's aid
with arguments borrowed from Wycliffe. But a compromise or understanding was afterwards arrived at,
and the Archbishop was persuaded to take up a con-
ciliatory line of policy with regard to Hus, if Wenzel on
his part would act with greater moderation towards the
clergy. Zbynek however died in the autumn of 1411
before the arrangement had been carried into effect.

The death of Archbishop Zbynek removed the personal element in the controversy, and left it freer to
work in a more extended field. The ques-

*Development
of Wycliffism
in Bohemia.*

tion up to this time had been the admissi-
bility of Wycliffe's teaching ; it now became
the application of that teaching to the larger problem
which arose out of the religious disorder of Bohemia, the
distracted state of Christendom at large, the division
in the Papacy, and the individual actions of John the
Twenty-third. Pope John soon gave an opportunity
for this new expansion of Wycliffism. Before the end
of 1411 he issued indulgences to promote a crusade, or
in other words to promote his Italian schemes ; and
Hus, in mind of Wycliffe's attack upon the English
crusade in Flanders thirty years earlier, raised an ener-

getic protest against the act and the whole theological basis on which it rested.   In June, to the alarm
of the University, he held a public disputation on the subject, in which Jerome of Prague
eagerly joined ; the younger students, in the enthusiasm of freshly excited zeal, led the latter in triumph
through the city.   The whole place was in an uproar,
sermons preached in support of the Pope's bull of indulgence were angrily interrupted, and in a few days
matters reached such a pitch that the bull was carried
about in a mock procession and finally burned.   King
Wenzel now became aware that, whatever his private
feeling in the contest, he must take measures against
these unruly proceedings.   The law was brought into
execution, and three men who had openly protested
against the preaching were put to death in spite of
Hus's attempts to secure their reprieve.   But the
popular excitement was only kindled anew, and it
was considered prudent to liberate others who had
been imprisoned during the late riots.

Just before this commotion Hus's enemies in the
theological faculty of the University had shown their
strength by repeating the condemnation of the forty-
five articles of Wycliffe, together with six others
ascribed to Hus, and further by persuading the King
to confirm and enforce their sentence.   Hus in consequence, however much he might possess the support
of the Bohemian people at large, could no longer claim
that of official authority.   His opposition to the indulgences made it inevitable that John the Twenty-third
should abandon his previous policy of moderation
towards him.   He now deputed a cardinal to reëxamine

1412.

the charges against Hus, with the result that the greater excommunication was pronounced against him, and

Hus subjected to the major excommunication. followed by a second bull which commanded that his person should be seized and that he should be handed over to the spiritual authority to be burned; the chapel of Bethlehem was to be destroyed. Hus, who indeed seems to have been in no danger, replied by an appeal to the sentence of a general council, and in the end to that of his supreme judge, Jesus Christ. The King however advised him to withdraw from Prague; and, for this reason and to save his friends trouble,—not in the least from any thought of cowardice,—before the end of the year 1412 he disappeared from public notice.

He remained in his retreat far away in the country for nearly two years, and visited Prague but seldom and

His journey to Constance. only in secret; until at last the assembly of the Council of Constance required his attendance there to take his trial before a body whose decision might be felt to represent the sober judgement of all Western Christendom. He was not indeed under any bodily compulsion to appear and defend himself; but he saw rightly that such a course was essential to the eventual success of his aims. He was careful to obtain an official certificate of his orthodoxy before leaving Bohemia. Then in October 1414 he set out on his journey towards Constance, and was afterwards provided with a liberally expressed safe-conduct from Sigismund, the King of the Romans, ensuring him against molestation on his going and returning as well as during his stay at Constance. Much has been written upon the subject of this document, and it has repeatedly been stated that Sigismund's acquiescence in Hus's condemnation involved a grievous breach of faith towards him. On the other hand it has been maintained that a safe-conduct, as such, could promise protection to an accused person on his way to trial, during the time of the trial, and in the event of his acquittal on his return journey, but could not interfere with the consequences of his condemnation. Neither of these assertions can be admitted in its entirety. The latter is excluded by the fact that it was never referred to at the time, even when the argument would have been most convenient; while as to the former, considering that Sigismund gave the safe-conduct to one whom he knew to lie under excommunication and yet added no words of reservation to the protection offered to Hus, as was usual in cases of the kind, it may be presumed that he believed he had power to defend him. When therefore he suffered Hus to be imprisoned and then carried out the sentence of the council upon him, Sigismund appeared to be guilty of treachery. Yet we may doubt whether he was aware of the usage which placed a spiritual offender wholly beyond the protection of any lay authority; and it has been well pointed out that Germany and especially Bohemia knew so little about the Inquisition and the systematic rules according to which heresy was dealt with, that surprise and indignation were excited by the application to Hus's case of the recognised principles of the canon law. 'The council could not have done otherwise than it did without surrendering those principles;'[1]

---

[1] H. C. Lea, *History of the Inquisition of the Middle Ages*, 2. 467 (1888).

but Hus none the less was convinced that at Constance he was under no personal risk. There was this simplicity in his character that he took things too literally, did not understand them as a man of the world would have done, but interpreted them for himself in the light of his own single-mindedness. He was thus deceived as to the extent of his protection, and complained bitterly when it was too late.

Hus was accompanied on the road to Constance by several Bohemian noblemen; he reached the place on the 3rd November. Before the end of the month the Pope and cardinals resolved that he should be put in prison, and after a brief hearing, which came to nothing, he was confined in the Dominican convent on an island in the lake. Sigismund on his arrival demanded Hus's release on the faith of his safe-conduct; but the Pope, the cardinals, and the council were obdurate. The truth was that, however earnestly Hus might urge, and probably urge with justice, that he was pure from the stain of heresy, the events which had happened in Bohemia were convincing to those who knew only their general purport, that there was a *primâ facie* case against him. The council felt that it was its duty to restore unity in Christendom, and nothing could be less conducive to this purpose than the dissemination of views and practices at variance with the general sentiment of Christians.

More than this, those who were in earnest in the cause of reform felt that their hopes of success would be gravely imperilled if there were a suspicion that under the name of reform there lurked a desire of

Imprisonment.

making far-reaching changes in the organic system of
the Church. In these circumstances a man with the
charges against him which were alleged against Hus
could not expect to go free. Besides this, a heretic
as such had been often decided authoritatively to be
beyond the protection of any temporal power. Sigismund thus was helpless to intervene in Hus's favour ;
and later on, in March, when Pope John's flight
might seem to give him the opportunity, he had learned
to acquiesce too completely in the action of
the council for it to be possible to take any
independent step.

1415.

Two successive commissions were appointed to examine into the opinions of Wycliffe and Hus. The
second reported on the 4th May condemning the forty-five articles from Wycliffe
which had been the cause of the controversy at Prague,
together with more than two hundred others which
had been supplied by the zeal of the University of
Oxford. Wycliffe's writings were ordered to be burned;
his bones were to be dug up and cast out.[1] This
famous decree, it was at once felt, involved in it the
fate of Hus, even though (as was the fact) he was free
from error on the cardinal point of the sacrament of the
altar. His friends renewed their protest against his
imprisonment, but without effect. They were answered
by a promise of Hus's speedy trial. On the 5th June
he was heard, but the case was already hopeless. Each
side was reasoning from a different set of premises, and
divided also on the first principles of philosophy ; and
Hus's general view of the nature of the Church and of

*His examina-
tion,*

---

[1] See above, p. 111.

the priesthood—a view which he had borrowed in its entirety from Wycliffe—was by itself sufficient to convict him, even though that view might be adequately supported by arguments from the fathers and from certain portions of the canon law. For two days more, on the 7th and 8th, he was heard at length. The council did all it could to induce him to submit to its judgement; but Hus, though fully persuaded of his complete orthodoxy, felt that as to recant anything which he believed was impossible, so to accept a form of statement which was not his own, would be to play his conscience false, while charges which had been wrongly brought against him he could not abjure because he had never held. It became almost a wrangle about words: Hus urged that he would defend nothing obstinately but would submit to better instruction; the council maintained that he must abjure without qualification everything that had been charged against him. And out of this miserable dispute, in which and condem- neither side could, and one side would not, nation. understand the other, came the fatal act by which Hus was condemned to death. On the 6th July he received his sentence, was degraded from his orders, and handed over to the secular arm. He was straightway led without the city into a field where the stake was ready. For the last time he was besought by the Palsgrave Lewis of Bavaria to make his peace with the Church; but he, who had always (we know) desired to die for the truth, once more repeated his willingness—'I am ready to die in that truth of the Gospel which I have been taught and written;'—and so, chanting his prayer for mercy from the office for

the Burial of the Dead, the flames were kindled about
him. Thinking to extinguish heresy, the Council of
Constance had made it the national faith of Bohemia,
and had made the martyr Hus the national hero and
the national saint.

CHAPTER XII.

THE END OF THE FIRST REFORM MOVEMENT.

THE Council of Constance had now carried out two out of the three objects for which it was assembled. It had deposed Pope John the Twenty-third; a few weeks later Gregory the Twelfth abdicated; and Benedict the Thirteenth maintained an obscure, and daily more insignificant, position in Spain. It had also, as it believed, put down heresy by the death of Hus, followed as this was in the following spring by the trial and death of his most active disciple Jerome of Prague. What remained was to choose a new Pope and to set on foot some effective scheme of reform. It was really the earnestness with which an important party in the council laboured for this end, that had operated most to Hus's prejudice. The council had presumed to cast out the Pope: some of its members stood committed to opinions involving more than a merely personal change in the Papacy; to some of them it seemed desirable that the position of the Papacy must undergo certain modifications, must submit to certain restraints, in order to command the obedience of Europe. How much the more anxiously must they avoid giving

1415.

Question of Reform.

countenance to any movement which threatened to
undermine the foundations not of the Papal only but
of the priestly power itself. Men like Ailly, the Cardinal of Cambray, proclaimed the preëminence of the
Church as above the Pope, just because it was essential
to the carrying out of the objects of the council. But
they had not a thought of attacking the mediæval
Church system in a vital part. By their assent to the
condemnation of Hus they had now proved that their
proposals of reform were not to overpass the limits of
correct Churchmanship; and to this business they at
once proceeded when the preliminary obstacles had, as
we have seen, been removed. But the very fact that
the most pressing work of the council had been accomplished made it all the harder to secure unanimity
about the further measures to be pursued.

Sigismund almost immediately quitted Constance
on a great tour of pacification. His aims were of
the most comprehensive kind: Europe was
to be united by his mediation to form a
grand crusade against the advancing power of the
Turks. But the year of the battle of Azincourt,
when France beyond this was torn between
two rival factions, was hardly a propitious
moment for so ambitious a scheme. It insensibly
narrowed itself and assumed a practical character.
First the Emperor went to Perpignan to make terms
with Benedict; Benedict himself was obdurate, but
the King of Aragon agreed that Spain should send
its representatives to the council. In the following
March Sigismund was at Paris, in May in London.
After his alliance with Henry the Fifth concluded at

July 18, 1415.

Sigismund's
negotiations.

Canterbury in August he returned to the Continent, and reached Constance again in January 1417. In these days of rapid communication we can hardly imagine a council sitting aimlessly through a year and a half of comparative suspense. It had been wrangling about the order of proceedings; each nation had its own grievances which appeared to it of chief moment, and was anxious to give them an opportunity of early discussion. Then new combinations of party were formed, and the alliance which Sigismund had made with England had the natural effect of drawing the French towards the Italian side. In the July after his return the council at last took the positive step of declaring Benedict no longer Pope. A committee was then appointed to set about measures of reform; but it had hardly been named before its work was practically superseded by the proposal that a new Pope should be first elected, and the election of a Pope, it was evident, might, and probably would, frustrate the power of the council for further action. But the council was excusably weary of the protracted debating, which seemed to have no definite end, of various and discordant plans.

1415-1417.

In September the death of Robert Hallam, Bishop of Salisbury, deprived the English nation of its leader and Sigismund of one of his main supporters. A month later, Henry Beaufort, Bishop of Winchester, and afterwards cardinal, appeared at the council; and his arrival coincided with the decision of the English nation to throw in their lot with the Italian party. Probably Henry the Fifth had been made aware of the hope-

1417.

Surrender of policy by the English nation.

lessness of carrying a struggle in which parties were
so evenly balanced to a successful conclusion, unless the
council were to sit for ever ; and his half-brother was
sent to effect the change of front with as little irritation to the Germans as could be avoided. Yet one
cannot but feel that the death of Bishop Hallam was an
important, if not a vital, element in the success of this
manœuvre. The English abandoned the Germans ; by
the beginning of October they had no choice but to
acquiesce in the immediate election of a Pope. Even
the stipulation that the Pope should be bound to set
about the work of reform without delay, was not accepted ; and the council, contenting itself with the
decree that future councils should be held every five
years (the next however being in seven years), formulated a basis for the election of the Pope. On the
30th October this was arranged : the Pope who should
be chosen was to coöperate in the task of reforming
the Church in a variety of matters enumerated under
eighteen heads, and this before the council should be
dissolved ; he was to be elected by the cardinals together with six nominees of each of the nations. On
Election of the 11th November the electors met and
Martin V. chose the Roman Cardinal Oddo Colonna, a
poor man though of illustrious family, of high character,
who took the title of Martin the Fifth.

The council had now sat all but three years, and
every one was weary and anxious to find a colourable
excuse for considering its work completed. After the
new Pope had repeated the condemnation of the errors
of Wycliffe and Hus, and the council had disposed of
some of the least controverted and least important

questions of reform, it was arranged that the rest of
the eighteen articles should be dealt with by means of
separate conventions or ' concordats' with the different
nations, a plan which was devised not less to minimise
the weight and value of the future concessions, than
to save the friction which had long become intolerable
through the jealousy of the component elements of the
council.   The consequence was that the concordats
proved little better than illusory; the reforms were
small in the present, though a prospect of more was
offered in the future : but even those who had been
earnest in their advocacy of reform were content to
leave their labours unfinished in the hope that the
next council (for this was a fixed engagement agreed
upon by the Council of Constance) would be better
able, with the ground freer, to work for the common
good of Christendom.   So the Council of Constance
Dissolution of   was dissolved on the 22nd April 1418.
the Council of   It was succeeded by that of Pavia in 1423,
Constance,
1418.   afterwards removed to Siena; but this was
too much wanting both in representative character
and authority to effect anything of importance.   The
conciliar movement was in danger of dying out when
it was revived by the assembly of the Council of Basle
in 1431, and the Council of Basle was only called
because the state of affairs in Bohemia was too urgent
to brook longer delay.

The last years of the Council of Constance display a
painful contrast to the enthusiasm and vigour with
End of the   which it had been heralded and opened.
Great Schism. Its tangible results were seen, it is true,
in the reunion of the Papacy.   Martin the Fifth was

at once accepted by most, and very soon he had no
rival to contend with. John the Twenty-third submitted in June 1419, was made a cardinal, and died
soon after; while the history of Benedict's succession in Spain exhibits the disintegrating tendency of
schism on a truly microscopical scale. When he died
in 1424 three of his cardinals elected their Pope,
Clement the Eighth, and one chose his own private
Pope, Benedict the Fourteenth. Five years after
Clement was appeased by the bishoprick of Majorca,
while Benedict as late as 1432 was thought worth
imprisoning and sending to Pope Martin.

But the gain of restored unity in the head of
Christendom had to be set against a state of things
rapidly assuming the dimensions of a civil
war in Bohemia. On Wenzel's death in
1419 Sigismund succeeded, and had to face
the revolt of his capital; within two years he was
driven from the country. The reforming party among
the Bohemians was acting in a spirit of vengeance for
the death of their chief. They poured into the monasteries, wrecked every image and relique, and handled the
monks or friars with the ferocity of religious hatred.
Often they put them to death, sometimes by burning.
Nothing was safe from the outrages of this fanatic—or
drunken, if the monks speak true—rabble; no place
was sacred to them. The most beautiful churches with
their choicest ornaments were burned without remorse.
Everything that marked the influence of German art or
Catholic allegiance was the prey of this puritan frenzy.
Slavonic patriotism combined readily with the forces of
religious zealotry, and the Hussites for a while domi-

nated the land. But they soon split into two divisions, which agreed in their common attitude of
resistance to Catholic control, but differed as to the
means by which their opposition should be carried
into effect. The moderate party were called Calixtins
(or Utraquists) because they allowed the *cup* to the
laity in the Lord's Supper; and these represented
fairly the opinions of Hus himself. The others fell
into several branches, united only by their common
policy of war; the extreme section among them not
only accepted without reserve the tradition of Wycliffe, including his denial of transubstantiation, but
went on into a variety of strange beliefs and practices, some visionary, some materialistic, which
threatened the success of their more sober brethren.
These, the orthodox members of the radical party
among the reformers, banded themselves round their
leader John Žižka, who united first-rate abilities as a
warrior and military organiser with a profound earnestness in the faith of Hus. His camp at Tabor furnished
not only a rallying-point for those who came to glory
in the name of Taborites, but a strong place of defence,
which held its ground victoriously until after a long
-and desolating war the radical party among the reformers, under Žižka's successor Procopius the Great,
was crushed at the battle of Lipan in 1434.

Before this the Council of Basle had received dele-
gates from Bohemia and had sought to bring them
over by patient hearing and argument. Cardinal
Giulano Cesarini, legate in Germany and president of
the council, showed an earnest desire to be concili-
atory and a generosity of spirit which communicated

itself to others; for he was known for the saintliest
churchman of his time, and in all ways beyond reproach. The general moderation and good temper
of these proceedings compare most favourably with
those which had led up to the condemnation of Hus,
and the absence of any thought of vindictive measures
shows that the world had learned something at least
from the lessons of Constance, though the dread of
Hussitism as a militant and extending power in Europe
may not have been without influence in counselling
moderation.   At the council itself no definite result
was arrived at; but further negotiations led
_{1433.} to a concession, within certain limits, of the
practice of administering the communion to the laity
in both kinds, as well as a compromise, rather of words
than of reality, in regard to the other Bohemian demands touching discipline over moral offences, the
license of preaching, and the possession and use of
temporal goods by the clergy.   Sensible of the toler-
ance and good intentions of the council, the moderate
advocates of reform were ready to unite with the con-
servative nobility to put an end to the struggle; and
a year later the Taborites suffered their final defeat,
which left them no longer an influential party, far less
a national force, in Bohemia.

Yet the extreme views to which the Czech movement had tended left their memorial not only in Bohemia (where the extreme reformed party emerge again
in a few years as the ' Unitas Fratrum,' or Bohemian
Brethren, by us best known as the Moravians), but
in Germany and beyond Germany; for it was to this
impulse that the Waldensian communities in Dau-

phiné and Piedmont owed their characteristic features. The old belief that the Waldenses (or Vaudois) re-

Influence of the Hussite movement on the Waldenses.

present a current of tradition continuous from the assumed evangelical simplicity of the primitive Church has lost credit since a critical examination of their literature has placed beyond a doubt the fact that it contains no element of anything but a Catholic nature which is earlier than the time when the Bohemian, and above all the Taborite, influence is known to have been excited in the Waldensian valleys. It is known, indeed, that the Waldenses excited the suspicion of the Catholics and subjected themselves to the rigour of the Inquisition by certain views which implied a disparagement of the value of holy orders, maintaining that laymen might, if necessary, perform sacerdotal functions, and that the efficacy of the ministration of the sacrament depended on the virtue of the celebrant. But otherwise the imagined primitive Christianity of these Alpine congregations can only be deduced from works which have been shown to be translations or adaptations of the Hussite manuals or treatises. The special Protestant tenets of the Waldenses are therefore not of native growth; and the sole point in which they are held by competent scholars to have influenced the later course of the reformation, lies in the fact that they had a version of the Bible in their vernacular. It is possible that this version may be the original from which the early German Bibles were translated; but the connexion is not yet proved, the balance of learned opinion is against it, and even if it were proved it would not follow that the Waldensian movement was in any respect hostile to the Catholic tradition. For in France a version of the Bible was set on foot in the thirteenth century, just as in England some parts of it were translated long before Wycliffe's time.

The Council of Basle had been summoned, as we have seen, to cope with the Bohemian difficulty; but The Council of Basle. when its prudent concessions had been effectual in confining the influence of that movement within the limits of Bohemia, and when its most pressing work seemed accomplished for it by the overthrow of the Taborites, the council, which from the outset had been thwarted by the Pope, turned its energy towards the aim of establishing a permanent control over him, an aim which involved an irreconcilable conflict with the Papacy. The positive results of the sessions of the two following years are found in a variety of resolutions dealing with the morals of the clergy, freedom of election in churches, disputed questions relating to the patronage of benefices, the restriction of appeals and of interdict, and the reduction of the number of the cardinals; above all a heavy blow was struck at the Pope's resources by the abolition of the right to levy *annates* or dues on appointment to a benefice. Extreme as these measures were, they received at the time no small measure of support outside the council. In 1438 Charles the Seventh of France, by the Pragmatic Sanction of Bourges, recognised the authority of the council and placed the essential points of its decrees, in particular the abolition of *annates*, on a legal footing in France. The opportunity for keeping money from passing out of the country was too valuable to be lost. In Germany

also, a year later, the Diet of Mentz published a law
of a like purport.   Both countries were disposed to
gain their own practical objects by much the same
method as that arranged in the concordats of the
Council of Constance.

But Eugenius the Fourth, the successor of Martin
the Fifth (who had died in 1431), considered not

Eugenius IV.   inexcusably that in this course of action the
very existence of the Papacy was at stake.
He ordered the dissolution of the council; and when
the fathers at Basle not only declined to follow him, but
pronounced him contumacious and resolved upon his
suspension, he held an independent council of his own
at Ferrara; then transferred it in 1439 to Florence,
and was able to effect what appeared to be the signal
success—though in fact it was only successful for
a moment — of reuniting the Greek Church in the
Catholic communion.   Meanwhile the obstinate Council of Basle decreed the Pope's deposition, and chose
an Antipope.   The truth was that neither was it strong
enough to coerce the Pope, nor the Pope to coerce it.
But insensibly Eugenius gained the day.   After a time
of hope, and then an interval of uneasiness, the Antipope Felix the Fifth faded into a nonentity, and in
little more than eight years after his election he was
glad to abdicate.   Long before this the council was
dying of exhaustion, and it came to an end almost
simultaneously with Felix' abdication at the beginning
of 1448.   What it had really proved was the incompatibility of the conciliar system with the accepted
position of the Papacy.

This incompatibility had not come into clear light

in the Council of Constance, because its business was to see to the removal of the existing Popes and then to set up another who should carry out the principles which it laid down. It dealt rather with what should be in theory the Pope's relations to the council, than what they were in fact. For until the election of Martin the fathers at Constance had no occasion to consult the personal wishes or policy of any Pope, and Martin was too wise to begin his pontificate by raising objections. He had submitted to certain restrictions for a prescribed space of five years : and when the time was over he was all the freer to exercise as complete a prerogative as any of his predecessors. This power he handed on to Eugenius ; and Eugenius was a man who, whatever his faults of temper, knew how to use his opportunities and to avail himself of the blunders of his antagonists. Greatly as men desired to see the limits of the Papal authority defined, especially in its relation to the Churches of the different countries, they were not prepared to support the council in reducing that authority to a shadow or in binding its exercise by impossible conditions. And when the council went on to compromise itself by the creation of a new schism, its failure became a certainty ; and its failure involved not only the collapse of the conciliar movement but also a steady reaction in favour of the Papal system. In the very year of the dissolution of the council the con-
1448. cordat of Vienna abolished the Mentz decrees, and with minor modifications left things as they had been. The progress of the change of feeling is marked, step by step, in the career of a clever Italian, Æneas Sylvius Piccolomini, afterwards Pope Pius the Second,

C. H. M

then a layman and a libertine, who from an eloquent
supporter of the council and secretary to its Antipope,
passed into the service of the Emperor Frederick the
Third, and manœuvred his policy with the view of restoring harmonious relations with the Pope, not without regard to contingent advantages to the secretary.
But Æneas Sylvius is only a type of the class of
diplomatists developed in the tedious wrangle between council and Pope, in which larger views and
nobler aims degenerated into vain personal self-
seeking.

Eugenius died, February 23, 1447, before he could
witness the completion of his hopes; but his successors were able to secure the fruits of the victory for a
long course of years.   The victory was won at a heavy
cost both for the Popes and for Christendom ; for the
Papacy recovered its ascendency far more as a political
than as a religious power.   The Pope became more than
ever immersed in the international concerns of Europe,
and his policy was a tortuous course of craft and in-
trigue, which in those days passed for the new art of
diplomacy.   In Italy itself, where a few states were
consolidating themselves at the expense of their smaller
neighbours, the Pope was more than ever a temporal
prince, guiding his actions by the rules of license and
overreaching as his rivals.   While too his spiritual
position seemed to be quite obscured, his temporal
supremacy itself was menaced by a perpetual entanglement with political affairs, in which he had no choice
but to act as an equal among equals, as an ally with
allies.   The Papacy survived as the ruler of the States
of the Church ; but in this quality alone it was evident

that its claims over Christendom at large could not be long sustained. To revert to a basis of spiritual domination lay beyond the vision of the energetic princes, the refined *dilettanti*, the dexterous diplomatists, who sat upon the chair of St. Peter during the age succeeding the Council of Basle. Of signs of uneasiness abroad they could not be quite ignorant; but they sought to divert men's minds from the contemplation of so perplexing a problem as Church reform, by creating or fostering new atmospheres of excitement and interest which might take the place of a current of thought that would only lead to trouble and disturbance ; or at best (if we may adopt the language of their apologists) they took advantage of the literary and artistic movement then active in Italy as a means to establish a higher standard of civilisation which might render organic reform needless.

Feeling thus that the agency of councils was discredited in the eyes of Europe, and reluctant to take action themselves, the Popes threw themselves with whole heart into the interests of the day. Nicolas the
_{Nicolas V.} Fifth, who followed Eugenius, devoted himself
_{1447-1455.} to that which was becoming the absorbing study and well-nigh the religion of Italy, the love of classical learning and classical antiquities,—in a word, humanism. But public affairs could not leave him quite to himself and his works of art. The onward progress of the Turks was a threat to Western civilisation such as no invasion had been since the Mongol advance of the thirteenth century ; and it became the Pope to stand forth as the leader in repelling the danger. In 1444 the Turks were met by a Hungarian

army, with a band of crusaders from other countries, led by Cardinal Cesarini. Overpowered by numbers, the Christians were utterly defeated and Cesarini slain. In nine years the victory was followed up by the conquest of Constantinople, and a panic fear seized upon the Latin world. Pope Nicolas at once proclaimed a crusade; but the Emperor Frederick the Third was feeble and poor, and the forces of Germany—the country to be threatened next—were divided by jealousy. It was not until 1456,

Calixtus III.

when Callixtus the Third was Pope, that the war of defence was seriously undertaken; and then the success of the crusaders in beating back the Turks from Belgrade was decided more by the heroic ardour of John Hunyadi and the Franciscan Saint John Capistrano than by the military support of Christendom.

Pius II.
1458-1464.

Once more in the pontificate of Pius the Second there was a real attempt to carry out a crusade, but the enterprise was not matured until 1464, and was stopped at the moment of departure by the death of the Pope who accompanied it. It is almost an irony that the Pope, who stands as the model of the secular man of letters of his time, should have died a martyr to a crusade; but there are no good grounds for questioning his sincerity of purpose. He knew what was expected of him as Pope, and he did it; further into his motives it is needless to go: he has at least the credit of setting on foot the last crusade. From his death the project was no more seriously discussed. It might be made use of as a pretext of policy or an instrument of taxation; but in the future war against the Turk ceases to rank among religious wars heralded and led by the Pope.

The Popes were content to reduce their range of activity, as much as might be, to Italy. Nicolas and Pius had united themselves completely with the Italian

Paul II.
1464-1471.

spirit of their day ;—Paul the Second only so far departed from it that his taste was for art for its own sake, and not for classical learning because it was the fashion ;—it was but a step to pass

Sixtus IV.
1471-1481.

on and realise, with Sixtus the Fourth, the Pope's position as the leader of Italians ; and thus, as we have said, the Papal States became the principal object of his concern, and the Pope himself chiefly conspicuous as an Italian prince mixed up in all the intrigues and wrangles of his day. Living thus altogether in an Italian world, where spiritual aspirations were forgotten in the passion for an intellectual or artistic ideal, and where moral restraints were thrown aside in the pursuit of whatever appealed to the senses, the Pope was unaware or regardless of the course of religious feeling in other countries, which had given efficacy to the conciliar movement at its inception, and which, though impaired by its decline, had only suffered a temporary relapse, and was before long to resume its entire and masculine strength. The desire for reform grew up again while the Pope recked not of it, and in half a century became a force with which the Papacy with its present resources was powerless to reckon.

CHAPTER XIII.

RELIGIOUS REVIVAL IN SPAIN AND ITALY.

LONG after the ending of the Council of Basle the idea of calling yet another council was repeatedly expressed.

Difficulty of the state of Chris- tendom.

The Pope might set himself against it; but still the suggestion, as the only expedient that had yet reached a practical stage, was again and again put forth in France and Germany; the condition of England was not such as to enable her to speak or even think with effect on the matter. But councils had sufficiently shown their impotence to touch the real issues, to remedy the real evils that affected the very being of Christendom; and it might even be doubted whether the Church itself, so deeply was every organ of it corrupted, had not outlived its day of vital ministry to mankind. That some change was necessary was clear to all religious men outside the immediate Papal environment; the only question related to the character and scope of the change. The truth was that all the complaints that had held their ground for above a century against the abuses inherent (as it seemed) in the Church system, had now more justification than ever. Not merely was the Church suffering from a general demoralisation which was traced to an evil system, but most of all to the evil example of its head; but it was now imperilled by a new influence, by the new devotion to the pagan classical world, which led in the minds of many to a frank avowal of disbelief in Christianity altogether. This temper of mind had its representatives, was even becoming fashionable, among high dignitaries of the Church. It became all the more important to keep the desire for reform separate in a marked way from those movements which had fallen under the censure of Christendom at Constance and Basle; it was the more necessary to show that what was aimed at was the purifying of the Church from acknowledged abuses, not the introduction into it of modes of thought that might open the way to erroneous beliefs and practices.

In one country alone of Europe was such a reform taken in hand officially and carried into complete execution. This was in Spain, where the long Spain. crusade against the Moors had kept alive a burning Catholic zeal which entitled the Spaniards to an exceptionally indulgent treatment from the Holy See. A century earlier they had secured for themselves privileges with regard to the taxation of the clergy and in restraint of their separate jurisdiction, which were sought in vain by other countries. Papal patronage and Papal interference in Spanish causes had also been curtailed, though not abolished. What England attempted to do by statutes of Provisors and Præmunire was accomplished to its full extent in Spain; and it was accomplished because there could be no doubt of the Catholic loyalty of the nation. For the same reason Ferdinand of Aragon and Isabella of

Castile, when they united the two crowns, were able
to carry on the work to completion. Their religious
character and hearty devotion to the interests
of the Church were above suspicion ; and
they were therefore the freer to exercise such a degree
of control over Church matters as would scarcely have
been tolerated in another country. Side by side with
their measures of administrative reform, their great
aim was to restore the Church, which laboured from the
common vices of the age, to a state of effective useful-
ness. They obtained the further limitation of the Pope's
powers of patronage. Sixtus the Fourth engaged himself to nominate to the higher benefices in Spain only
such natives of the country as the Crown should approve ; and the non-resident foreigner was gradually
driven out from all benefices alike. Besides this, it
was ordained that all Papal bulls relating to the legal
rights of private persons should not acquire validity
until they had passed through an official examination.
The Church-courts also were brought into closer relation
with the civil power; and the Church subjected to taxation for civil purposes even from its spiritual revenues.

Of not less importance were the measures taken for
the reform of Church discipline. Among those who
were chiefly active in this work Cardinal
Ximenez was the most influential. His
aim was that Church offices should be given only to
men qualified by their religious and moral rectitude.
Himself a friar of rigorous observance, he carried his
code of duty into all his practical public life. He
corrected the abuses of the monasteries by repeated
visitations ; he removed worldly and profligate church-

1479.

Cardinal
Ximenez.

men from their benefices, and made use of the royal patronage to appoint bishops whose learning and piety were beyond reproach. But the low standard of education among the clergy at large could not be advanced in a moment. Ximenez set himself in earnest to promote this end by the foundation of new colleges and by the extension of old ones, with special theological advantages ; and the fruit of his labours was seen in the goodly band of Spanish divines who illustrated the Catholic Church in the following century.

But if we have laid a stress upon the national character and religious spirit of the Spanish reformation under Ferdinand and Isabella, we must not forget that Spanish Christianity was still of necessity animated by a militant or crusading zeal. It was these sovereigns who, while they were carrying on the last war of extermination against the Moors, determined once for all to clear the land already theirs of unbelief by the expulsion of the Jews ; and in ten years the last Mussulman was driven from Spain. Before this a new weapon was placed in the hands of the Spanish rulers with the authorisation of Pope Sixtus the Fourth, by the institution of the Holy Office of the Inquisition. This was primarily an ecclesiastical court to examine doubtful or heretical opinions, and it punished offenders as a rule with spiritual penalties : if it condemned them to punishment in life or limb, its execution was remitted to the civil magistrate. In this manner the connexion between Church and State was kept as close as possible : both were united as the defenders of Catholic orthodoxy.

1482–1492.

1480.

In Spain the new ardour for the study of ancient
learning had not operated as an unsettling influence
Humanism on men's minds; the humanists there had
turned themselves as though naturally to
theological activity : it was Cardinal Ximenez himself
who brought out the first polyglot Bible, the apt symbol
of the union of the old studies with the new method.
In Italy on the other hand the re-discovery of Greek
in Italy. had an effect upon cultivated men not unlike that of the revolution in natural science
which marks the past century ; only the modern tendency was to find in the concrete processes of nature
that key to all the problems of human existence which
the men of the fifteenth century found in the literature
of ancient Greece : both alike led to the depreciation
or denial of the Christian revelation.   At Florence,
the intellectual capital of Italy, — above all while
Lorenzo de' Medici presided 'magnificently' over the
policy, tastes, fashions, and amusements of his fellow-
citizens,—the excitement roused by humanism answered to a general indifference in matters of religion.   While open distaste for the forms of the
Church was decently avoided, it was not the less
clear that the faith which they represented had died
out among the educated Florentines.   A few curious
thinkers—honest Christians withal—sought to reconcile the Greek and the Christian, the pagan and the
mediæval, by a philosophical system drawn from the
Neo-Platonist school of Alexandria.   Such were Marsiglio Ficino and his disciple Giovanni Pico della
Mirandola.   They thought they were merely reëstab-
lishing Plato in his rank of the chief of philosophers

from which he had been ousted in the Middle Ages by Aristotle; but when they had once admitted the principle of comprehension, the temptation to overpass the bounds of sobriety was too exciting to be resisted, and Pico extended the sphere of his speculation by absorbing elements from the Jewish cabbalistic tradition and from the mysterious regions of astrology and magic. Evidently, noble as was their desire of restoring the unity of human thought, these whole-hearted philosophers failed through lack of the critical gift. At most their views could appeal to a very select circle, and the risk they ran was shown by the narrowness with which Pico escaped the consequences of a Papal censure.

To a religious churchman indeed these constructive efforts of the humanists might seem more objectionable than the evil which they were aimed to meet; for indifference was after all a negative fault, while these philosophers were supplanting the accredited beliefs of Christendom by a positive system of their own. The reäction is shown by the work and teaching of Girolamo Savonarola. A Dominican friar of the convent of San Marco in Florence, Savonarola preserved in the midst of that vain and worldly city a rigour of life, a purity of soul, and an unquenchable missionary zeal which forced him into action. But it cost him many years of hard striving before he found the power to make his voice heard. He thirsted to change the hearts and unruly lives of his fellow-men; preached to them with an eloquence which was all the more startling to the Florentines because it gained nothing from the

Savonarola,

b. 1452.

1490.

literary arts that seemed to them a part of their very
being. He urged them to do penance for the sins of the
city, and a multitude answered to the call. He warned
them as a prophet of the doom hanging over them, and
mastered them with the spell of his denunciations.
To a large party among the Florentines he was at once
guide, guardian, father-confessor. If he denounced
the acts of the Popes, their manner of life, and the
sensual surroundings of their court, he could do it
with the greater freedom because in matters of faith
he was not only blameless but a pattern to all other
churchmen. If he attacked the house of the Medici,
it was because in his simple-minded way he traced
to their preëminence the vices into which Florentine
society had fallen.

But unhappily his hostility to the Medici made
him a party-leader and placed him in a position for
which his unworldliness and apocalyptic spirit wholly
unfitted him. Believing himself to be the chosen instrument of a vast moral and religious quickening of
Italian society, political aims became to him revealed
truth, policy was directed by prophecy. When the
French under Charles the Eighth entered the
land, they were the divinely appointed scourge
to chastise and purify it. Savonarola himself was one
of the embassy that went forth to meet Charles; and
when almost immediately afterwards the Medici were
driven forth from Florence, it was the party of Savonarola that rose to power. After a year the French
ingloriously retired; but Savonarola and the party
that followed him still held with France, and thus in-
vited the censure of Pope Alexander the Sixth, whose

1494.

chief aim at the time was to consolidate a league against that country. Florence was isolated, and must be brought back to common action with the rest of Italy; and Florence could be best attacked through the all-powerful preacher. Savonarola was first inhibited from preaching, then permitted to preach with a caution as to how he preached. But secure in the consciousness of divine guiding, and thinking nothing of his own safety, Savonarola advanced to a tone of reproach and threatening towards the Roman See which could only be answered by an excommunication. It was not so much that Pope Alexander cared for the friar's criticism as that this criticism reflected the Florentine opposition to his policy. Savonarola was excommunicated on the 13th May 1497; the magistrates of Florence laboured for his release, but finding their efforts fruitless they at last determined to brave the excommunication by inviting Savonarola to resume his preaching in the cathedral. The step was no doubt imprudent, for so public a disregard of Papal authority could not but weaken his following. Yet on the other hand the Pope was looked askance at by a large party at Florence, and his private reputation was so scandalous as to provoke a new desire for a general council to reform the Roman Court. That Charles the Eighth favoured such a proposal was natural on political grounds; Savonarola's support of it was simply the last form in which his ardent wish for the purification of the Church cast itself, but this support was fatal to any hope of mercy from the Pope.

Alexander urged the Florentines to restrain the obnoxious preacher, and, whether through his influence or not, a change of feeling soon gradually took place. The preaching was put a stop to; and though his friends still preached for him the re-action in Florentine opinion grew apace. On the 8th April 1498 his enemies took him prisoner, and he was brought to trial. A confession was drawn from him under torture, which acknowledged that he was a false prophet: how much of it was due to the weakness of the sufferer, and how much to the malice of his examiners, it is hard now to say. The Pope sent down commissioners, and Savonarola and two of his disciples were found guilty of heresy on the 22nd May. On the following day they were hanged on a gallows set up in the space before the Old Palace at Florence, and a fire then kindled beneath their bodies. The death of Savonarola was a judicial murder; but the charge of heresy was no essential part of his trial; it was, as it were, an after-thought, a convenient mode of introducing the Pope's authority at the conclusion. Savonarola was a victim of political expediency, while he believed —and in one sense believed rightly—that he was a martyr to religion. He has been truly described as ' a great moral reformer, who was driven at the last to take up the position of an ecclesiastical reformer also; but he followed the lines of Gerson and Ailli, and wished to take up the work which the Council of Constance had failed to accomplish. His conception of moral reform led him into politics, and his political position brought him into collision with the Papacy. Rather than abandon his work he was prepared to face a conflict with the Papacy, but his enemies were too numerous and too watchful, and he fell before their combined force.' [1]

March 1498.

[1] Creighton, *History of the Papacy*, 3. 247.

CHAPTER XIV.

REFORM IN GERMANY: THE LATERAN COUNCIL.

THE same needs and hopes which led to the purification of the Spanish Church and to the attempted·
reformation of Savonarola operated widely,
though for a time in a confused way, in
Germany. It was once usual to trace back the movement carried into effect by Luther to a long line of
forerunners— Mystics, Friends of God, Brethren of
Common Life. But in truth these earlier reformers
had little in common with their successors of the sixteenth century, or rather had nothing to separate them
from the corporate life of Christendom. They sought
but to realise in practice what all Christians professed.
They opposed nothing in the system of the Church,
only protested against admitted abuses. If they laid
peculiar stress upon the mystical elements in theology,
upon the emotional side of religion, they formed but
a school of thought and a religious order within the
Church. Now and then the mystic might be led into
extravagant speculations, but such was also the case
wherever metaphysical studies were pursued. Master
Eckehart in the fourteenth century has been held by
virtue of his German sermons to have occupied a

Early Pietism in Germany.

position analogous to that of Wycliffe, in so far as he gave himself up to spreading the gospel in the lower ranges of society by earnest popular preaching; but his Latin works which have lately been brought to light show him to have been a correct, if not a servile, disciple of Saint Thomas Aquinas. That his moral teaching and that of men like Tauler had the effect of heightening the current dissatisfaction at the evil state of the Church, need not be controverted; but the German Mystics led men in no sense into a mental attitude which could have adapted itself to the theological atmosphere of the reformers of the sixteenth century.

To quicken the sense of religion, to enforce the duty of personal holiness, this was the aim of the early German reformers. Side by side with them worked the Brethren of Common Life, who took their origin in the house founded by Gerard Groot at Deventer. They left the larger questions of reform in the Church system to be debated fruitlessly by councils, and occupied themselves with the task of teaching the reality of religion in their own circle. And the secret of their success lay just in the simplicity of their view and in their loyalty to the Church tradition. Not only did they draw numerous bands of followers into their body, but if the book *Of the Imitation of Christ,* attributed to Thomas of Kempen, be truly a production of one of their society,—the fact is not certain, but the work is known to have been widely circulated among them,—they may claim to have given to Christendom a manual of devotion which from the day it was produced until now has exercised an influence without rival among devout believers of every Church and

The Brethren of Common Life.

sect. Nor were such endeavours confined to particular local communities. In different parts of Germany there were vigorous steps taken, by means of visitations and by the personal efforts of single men, to bring the life and discipline of the monasteries more into accord with the principles of their foundation. Among those who laboured to this end no man was more strenuous than Nicolas Krebs of Cues, best known as Cusanus, who was made Papal legate in 1451 ; and he had been brought up in the community at Deventer. The spirit of the Brethren of Common Life thus worked in a wider sphere and became the motive force for the reformation of Church life in Germany.

Cusanus, who had attended the Council of Basle and had followed the varying policy of his friend Æneas Sylvius, represents also the new current of intercourse between Germany and Italy. All through the fifteenth century there was a constant passage of young Germans into Italy, eager to learn the classical erudition which was only to be acquired there. The reflexion upon their country is seen in the rapid growth of universities. In the fourteenth century Germany had but five universities,—Prague, Vienna, Heidelberg, Cologne, and Erfurt ;—by the first years of the following century the number had increased to seventeen. And though these foundations were directed according to the old traditions of school-learning, the influence of Italian humanism could not be shut out, and it quickly flowed by means of the younger men throughout the German lands from Louvain to Vienna, and from Basle to Rostock. But in Germany the spread of humanism

Spread of humanistic culture.

did not mean, as in Italy, the neglect or disparagement of theological learning. The great names of German humanism are the names of men such as Agricola and Reuchlin, who studied ancient literature with the purpose of bringing its resources to bear upon the knowledge and illustration of the Bible ; if they formed the minority among the teachers of the age, they still worked in harmony with their older-fashioned colleagues, and in this way succeeded in infusing the modern method of study with the less friction among their scholars. Nor must we forget in this connexion the revolution caused in the vehicle of literature by the Teutonic invention—whether it came from Haarlem or Mentz—of the printing-press, which in Germany particularly was made available for the purpose of that diffusion of religious knowledge which is characteristic of the earlier German reform-movement, as well as in the interest of general culture.

That the various streams of renewed religious activity and their spread among the people of Germany flowed by a natural course into the whirlpool of revolt against the Catholicism of Rome in the sixteenth century, can only be maintained subject to important reserves. The very age in which this activity manifested itself is conspicuous for its attachment to all the elements of popular worship and ceremonial against which the protestant reformers contended with greatest zeal,—the special reverence in which images and reliques were held, the devotion paid to the Blessed Virgin, the belief in current miracles :—at no time was the use of indulgences more common. Reforma-

tion as yet meant nothing else than the rëestablish-
ment of Catholic piety in its fulness. Yet it was
more and more felt that the reforms and advances
in religious life were rather the result of individual
effort than of any consciousness in the Church itself,
in a corporate sense, of its spiritual obligations. The
Church as an organisation did not gain in general respect. Increased intercourse with Italy brought back
stories of the condition of the Papal Court which were
not likely to make men more ready to contribute
towards its support or more loyal to it as the centre of
Christianity.

From criticism it was doubtless easy to pass on to
express opposition. The examples however which occur
of such opposition show by their very ineffectiveness
that the temper of the time was not yet ripe for decided
action. When John of Wesel, a theological teacher
of Erfurt University, frankly attacked the principle
of indulgences, a threat of prosecution soon moved
him to recant. John Wessel of Groningen, himself
brought up in the circle of the Brethren of Common
Life, taught an exclusive dependence upon the Bible
in matters of faith that reminds us of Wycliffe, and a
doctrine of justification that closely approaches Luther's;
while, as for the constitution of the Church, he would
restore it to the ideal of Christian community as he
believed he found this in the first ages of Christianity. But his own life was so simple and inoffensive
that he never provoked open hostility ; he spoke what
he believed, but had no ambition to lead a rebellion.
Beside these isolated appearances, there was doubtless
a continuous effort made by the Bohemian Brethen

to carry on a missionary work in Germany, and the extreme character of the doctrines of many of them with regard to society and to Church government made them doubtless acceptable to people of unsettled minds; but partly owing to the antagonism of Czech and Teuton the extent of their influence was circumscribed, and it is hazardous to attribute great significance to their operation.

The general impression left on the mind by a study of the religious state of Germany in the fifteenth century is that there were elements tending towards reform active in a wide area, but the reform aimed at was that about which there was no controversy; there were also elements wrought up through discontent at the evils in the existing Church system and impatience of ecclesiastical exactions, through the literal study of the Bible, and through the restlessness of spirit excited by the new humanism, which clearly pointed in the direction of a more penetrating change in the order things. But it is probably true that these latter forces had not acquired sufficient potency to work the change, but for the energy of a single man who reflected so accurately the temper of his countrymen that he was able to carry them with him a stage, or many stages, further than they would have desired to go but for such impulse.[1]

In England, where the Church was labouring under
England.   an accumulation of disorders not dissimilar
to those of Germany, humanism and theological study likewise moved together and inspired a few

---

[1] The history of the German Reformation is reserved for another volume in the present series.

teachers in the endeavour to give a new life and
reality to Christianity by a faithful following of the
Bible.   Among these John Colet, Dean of St. Paul's,
stood foremost, beside his disciple Erasmus.   But the
state of England was not favourable to the silent
movement of reform, and many as were those who
passed from such teachers at Oxford and Cambridge,
eager to impress their spirit upon England in the loyalty
of Catholic conviction, they were easily overpowered
when the great rupture came by the noisy multitude who
looked for favour from the new Head of the Church and
for profit from the institutions which he pillaged.   For
the reality of the protestantism of the first age of the
English Reformation is not of indigenous growth, but
transplanted from the protestantism of Germany.   It
was after the change was made that the English Reformers discovered their parentage in Wycliffe.

Ever since the end of the Council of Basle the
notion of summoning another general council was
The Council   constantly kept alive, whether in the hope
of Lateran.   of finding an effective instrument for the
correction of disorders in the Church, or for the purpose
of bringing pressure upon the Papacy, whose experience
of recent councils was not likely to make it view the
assembly of another with favour.   At last in the pontificate of Julius the Second, who followed Alexander
Sept.-Oct.   the Sixth (if we omit the four weeks' rule
1503.   of Pius III.), the crisis was brought about
by the action of some of the cardinals who were
opposed to the Pope.   They summoned and held a
1511.   council at Pisa, afterwards removed to Milan,
and Pope Julius thought it politic to answer the

rebellious cardinals by calling a council to meet at
the Lateran Palace in 1512. The Council of Milan
had cited the Pope, and on his non-appearance had
declared him suspended for contumacy : the Council
of the Lateran replied by pronouncing all the acts of
its rival null and void, and its supporters guilty of
schism. The political state of Italy at the time, apart
from the prestige inherent in a council held and presided over by the Pope, decided the victory, though
Julius himself did not live through the whole

1513.   of its sessions. His successor, Leo the Tenth,
Giovanni de' Medici, continued his Church policy,
and the council reassembled. The schismatic cardinals,
who had long since removed their council from Milan
to a safer distance at Lyons, made their submission,
and the Lateran Council set itself to its proper work.

What this work was is highly significant of the
intellectual results of the Renaissance in Italy. First
the council enforced the belief in the immortality and
individuality of the soul, and forbade clergymen to
spend more than five years in secular studies unless
they added to these the study of theology or canon
law. The question of reform in Church discipline,
especially with respect to the Curia, was next discussed,
adjourned, and again discussed and adjourned. The
bishops then proceeded to require a limitation of the
privileges of the monastic orders : the decision of this
controversy was also deferred. Decrees on certain
minor points were passed in 1515, but it was not
until, after a tedious delay, the council reassembled a
year later that Pope Leo felt strong enough in his
general political position to lead it to some sort of

effective action. Difficult matters were left on one side, and the council in its eleventh session issued a decree warning unlearned preachers to avoid subjects which might provoke scandal or involve danger. A question of political importance of the first magnitude was next dealt with, when the council annulled the Pragmatic Sanction which established the liberties of the Gallican Church. A concordat took its place by which the king Francis the First gained what the national Church lost. Finally the dispute concerning the exemption of monastic foundations was conciliated by a decree which enlarged the powers of the bishops and parish priests. Then on the 16th March 1517 the council was dissolved.

Except in the political victory over the French Church and the recalcitrant cardinals, the results of the council were insignificant. So little was thought of it that it passed unrecognised by the sovereigns of Europe, almost unnoticed in the diplomatic correspondence of the time. The really pressing matters of reform were left out of account, not merely because the members of the council were divided but because they felt that they were not sufficiently representative of the opinion of Christendom to give judgement upon them. The smallness, almost triviality, of the council's work might even be claimed as a justification for the intervention of some one outside the circle of ecclesiastical authority to take upon himself the duty which, however much admitted, that authority failed to accept. And the support which Luther won as the vindicator of that claim may be viewed as evidence of the popular recognition of the duty.

With the issues that followed we are not here concerned.   It is enough if the present sketch has at all
succeeded in making plain the process of history by
which the impulse given to religious enquiry by
Wycliffe passed, through Hus, into the consciousness of
reformers in a wider field.   Thus the reforming tradition
into which both Wycliffe and Hus entered and which
they helped to mature, came to form the essential
element in the aims of those who were their chief
opponents at the Council of Constance.   Through the
public opinion aroused by their efforts the conception
of a council acquired a vitality which outlived the
conciliar movement itself, and grew strong, in defiance
of the failure of the last council before the great rupture,
until it became transmuted into the conception of the
Church not as a universal monarchy with the Pope as
sovereign, but as a body coincident with and reflecting
the religious conscience of each separate nation.

INDEX.

———•◆•———

THE END.

DATE DUE

OCT 18 '79	MAY 7 '86		
OCT 22 '79	SEP 23 '86		
DEC 13 '79	OCT 29 '86		
JUL 11 '80	NOV 19 '86		
OCT 22 '80	DEC 11 '86		
NOV 19 '80			
JAN 21 1981			
MAY 15 '81			
SEP 21 '83			
OCT 12 '83			
OCT 17 '84			
NOV 7 '84			
DEC 12 '84			
DEC 21 '84			
NOV 27 '85			